C0-AVZ-512

SALVATION TOMORROW

SALVATION TOMORROW

by

STEPHEN NEILL

LUTTERWORTH PRESS
GUILDFORD AND LONDON

First published 1976

Quotations from the Revised Standard Version of the Bible are by kind permission of the Division of Christian Education of the National Council of the Churches of Christ in the United States of America copyrighted 1946, 1952, © 1971, 1973

ISBN 0 7188 2272 2

COPYRIGHT © 1976 STEPHEN NEILL

*Printed in Great Britain by
Cox & Wyman Ltd
London, Fakenham and Reading*

261.2
N317

7804226

CONTENTS

PREFACE   vii

INTRODUCTION   viii

1 WHERE ARE WE NOW?
1. 'Edinburgh 1910'   1
2. Darkening Horizons   5
3. The Century of Achievement   12
4. Penitent Churches   18

2 DIALOGUE WITH MEN OF OTHER FAITHS
1. A Shrinking World   22
2. Getting to Know   24
3. The Nature of Dialogue   32
4. Honesty and Decision   37
5. Less Easy than might be Supposed 40

3 A MORATORIUM ON MISSIONARIES?
1. Missionary, Go Home!   44
2. The Nature of the Christian Task   49
3. The Nature of the Church   51
4. The Nature of Mission   57
5. Identity with What?   63

4 REVOLUTIONARY ACTIVITY FOR ALL?
1. The Church and Politics   69
2. Politics and the Third-World Churches 74
3. To Make Oppression Bitter   78
4. Violence and Non-violence   87
5. The End of It All   96

5 TRAINING – FOR WHAT?
1. A Cry of Distress   100
2. Dangerous Places   104
3. No Other Road?   110
4. Where Does the Layman Come In? 114
5. And What of the Sheep?   119

6 GREATER THINGS THAN THESE

1. Prophets in Peril   125
2. What Next?   129
3. Towards the Twenty-first Century   136

PREFACE

The chapters contained in this volume, originally given as the Chavasse Lectures at Wycliffe Hall, Oxford, have been written and rewritten in the light of all that has been happening in the world and especially in the Fifth Assembly of the World Council of Churches held at Nairobi, the reports and documents of which have just come to hand.

Clearly it was impossible to include in so small a book all the subjects dealt with in many ecumenical gatherings. Some of special interest to myself, such as ecology and pollution, have simply been omitted. In accordance with the intention of the Chavasse Lectures, the main emphasis has been in the field of evangelism, or as 'Nairobi 1975' very suitably called it: 'Confessing Christ Today.'

I believe that the ecumenical cause is best served by critical study and by frank and friendly criticism of one another within the fellowship. I do not pretend to agree with everything that has been said and done in ecumenical circles in recent times. But I can record my whole-hearted agreement with the closing words of the best report that came out of Nairobi, that just referred to as 'Confessing Christ Today':

> We need to recover the sense of urgency . . . Confessing Christ must be done today . . . The world requires and God demands that we respond in all haste. 'And how terrible it would be for me if I did not preach the Gospel' (I Cor. 9:16).

And we can all join in the prayer sent out to the world from the Assembly:

> God of hope, whose Spirit gives light and power to your people, empower us to witness to your name in all the nations, to struggle for your own justice against all principalities and powers, and to persevere with faith and humour in the tasks that you have given to us. Therefore we cry together, *Maranatha; come, Lord Jesus.*

I owe a special debt of gratitude to Wycliffe Hall, where the lectures were first given, and which has since become my home.

Oxford 1976.

S.N.

INTRODUCTION

The Bangkok Assembly of the Department of Evangelism and World Mission of the World Council of Churches 'Salvation Today' was held in January 1973. That meeting was criticized on the ground that it made hardly any reference to salvation as that word is understood in the Scriptures; and that the theology to which it gave expression was not that of today but that of the day before yesterday.

Church history does not stand still, and much has happened in the period between Bangkok and the end of 1975.

First came the notable Congress on Evangelism organized at Durban by Mr. Michael Cassidy, and described by him in an interesting book, *Prisoners of Hope*. For many that gathering was the first experience of blacks and whites living together, and of the illumination and frustration to which such propinquity can give rise. A Congress which was addressed by Dr. Billy Graham, and at which the Bible Studies were given by Dr. Hans-Ruedi Weber of the World Council of Churches, was an event of more than local significance.

The next event was the Colloquy held at Geneva in September 1973, and duly recorded in the *International Review of Mission* for January 1974 (published by the WCC), at which almost for the first time representatives of the two wings mistakenly known as 'evangelical' and 'ecumenical' met for friendly discussion of points of agreement and difference.

Early in 1974 followed the Chicago Declaration put out by a number of American 'evangelicals' on the responsibility of the Christian in international and social affairs. This was significant as marking a return by evangelicals to concerns of their ancestors which more recent generations had seriously neglected.

And so to the Assembly convened in Lausanne in July 1974 by some sections of the leadership in the 'evangelical' cause. The Lausanne Covenant is verbose and gives evidence of haste in composition; but it is not polemical, and can well serve as a basis for discussion between 'evangelicals' and 'ecumenicals'.

These years have been marked, then, by notable convergence between groups which all acknowledge the same Lord, yet often find themselves diverging in their understanding of his will and his commands.

And so to the Fifth Assembly of the World Council of Churches, held in Nairobi in November and December 1975. The approach of this event had awakened a good deal of anxiety in the minds of old friends and supporters of the ecumenical movement.

The World Council in recent years has not been very good at listening to advice. It had been warned a great many times that a meeting of this kind demands careful preparation over at least three years, if it is to make any mark on the mind of either the church or the world. For this Assembly serious preparation began hardly a year before the event itself.

The Council had been reminded that an Assembly which meets for only fifteen days cannot deal effectively with more than one theological subject. Concentration is the parent of effectiveness. Nairobi 1975 tried to deal with six major themes, and in consequence produced reports which no one is likely to read except church historians anxious to find out what people were talking about in 1975.

It had been told very firmly that the delegates of the churches could not possibly do good work unless they were protected against the presence of visitors and others who had no official relationship to their work. At this Assembly the delegates were actually outnumbered by visitors, stewards, fraternal workers and others, who represented nothing and no one, and were considered by some to be a hindrance to the work that had to be done.

And yet things went much better than might have been expected. The importance of this Assembly was that the delegates of the churches made it plain that this was their Assembly. They would not accept docilely what had been prepared for them by the Central Office in Geneva. As far as the limitations of time allowed, they would make their voices heard, and would try to ensure that the Assembly was the mouthpiece of the churches, and not of any ecumenical establishment. No one could fail to note that these delegates were far more closely in touch with what is really happening in the world than many of those who had prepared the programme, though this is hardly surprising since it is they who are really doing the work of the churches.

So the Assembly did not do very much, and produced no striking document. The one good report is the first, 'Confessing Christ Today'. For all that the Assembly has probably saved the World Council of Churches from disintegration. The Council can live only as it is a Council of Churches. If the lesson of Nairobi is learned, the Council may recover some of the impetus and inspiration of its early years, and speak again in terms of a living church in daily confrontation with a living but sorely needy world.

1

WHERE ARE WE NOW?

1. 'Edinburgh 1910'

The first World Missionary Conference held at Edinburgh in 1910 was the beginning of many things, not least of the ecumenical movement in its modern form.

It has become a cliché that that Conference was held in a mood of colonial euphoria, at a time when the dominance of the western, and therefore allegedly Christian, nations over the rest of the world seemed almost absolute and unchallengeable. Undoubtedly some among the members of the Conference, and among the much larger number of those who supported them, thought in terms of a steady advance of the Christian message throughout the world, until by a process of irresistible expansion 'the earth shall be filled with the glory of God as the waters cover the sea'.

The Conference was dominated by its chairman, the American Methodist Dr. John R. Mott. Never far from the background of his thinking was the memorable slogan which he had coined and propagated far and wide: The Evangelization of the World in this Generation. I have never been able to fix the date at which Mott first made use of this expression. It cannot, I think, have been later than 1890. For the next thirty years and more this note was to be heard resounding in the corridors of power throughout a great part of the Protestant missionary enterprise. The phrase did not find universal acceptance. The doyen of missionary thinking in Germany, Gustav Warneck, steadily refused to pay attention to the careful distinction which Mott always drew between evangelization, the proclamation of the divine message, and conversion, the favourable response of man to that proclamation, and persisted in supposing that what Mott was putting forward was a facile American dream of the conversion of the whole world within the span of a single generation of human life. But not many people in the English-speaking world read German, and for the most part these

1

criticisms went unheard. Moreover as time went on Mott laid increasing emphasis on responsibility in the light of opportunity; it is the duty of each generation of Christians to see to it that, as far as lies within its power, the Gospel of Christ is preached to every single one of its contemporaries in the non-Christian world. The challenge was heard, and captured the minds of countless young Christians of that day and generation, who felt that a new dimension had been added to their understanding of the Christian faith.

If Mott presided over the Edinburgh Conference in a mood of optimism, he could well defend his position by drawing attention to what had happened in the century preceding the Conference. If Carey's 'pleasing dream' of a World Missionary Conference (to be held at the Cape of Good Hope in 1810) had come down out of the realm of dreams into that of sober reality, the Conference would have consisted of a small number of people drawn from very limited areas of the world. East Asia would have been unrepresented. There would have been no one from the Muslim countries. Africa would have been represented only by a small number of workers from scattered settlements in the coastal areas such as Sierra Leone. Those who came would have come no doubt filled with the high hopes of early morning; but the noonday fulfilment of those hopes would still have been far beyond their horizon. In 1910 Mott could point to at least ten reasons for confident expectation, and would have affirmed that optimism was an expression of reliance on the greatness of God and not merely the effervescence of purely human speculation:

1. The number of Christian witnesses in the non-Christian world had doubled and redoubled itself in the century. In 1810 missionaries had been numbered in tens. By 1860 this had grown to hundreds. In 1910 the number had to be counted in thousands, even if no account were taken of contemporary developments in the Roman Catholic world.

2. A century of almost unbroken peace had proved favourable to the development of the Christian cause. India, for example, had for the first time in its long history become politically unified under British rule, so that a man could walk from Cape Comorin to the Khyber Pass without crossing a frontier and with no more danger than might arise from the occasional

2

presence of wild beasts or robbers. The steady advance of colonial power had put an end to the tribal wars which had made up so much of the history of Africa in earlier centuries. China was less peaceful, yet the whole country had been opened up to western penetration. And so the tale went on, with little suspicion at the time that the story might look very different viewed through the eyes of those whose lands were being 'opened up' to alien forces from outside.

3. The progress of tropical medicine, including such epoch-making discoveries as the identification by Sir Robert Ross in 1894 of the process of the dissemination of malaria, had made it possible for the white man to live in reasonable health in areas previously rendered almost inaccessible by endemic disease.

4. The whole Bible had been translated into all the major forms of human speech, and the New Testament completed in many languages of lesser range. These translations were in many cases rough and uncouth, and showed all the imperfections of pioneer work in languages as yet imperfectly known. But the back of the work had been broken, and the way shown to those who would follow on to perfect the work of the pioneers.

5. There had been no form of religion, from the simplest up to the most sophisticated, which had not during the century yielded some converts to the Christian faith. Some religions had indeed shown themselves much more accessible than others to Christian propaganda. But even Islam, with its apparently impregnable certainty as to the bare unity of God, and the small community of the Parsis, shrouded in the mystery of their origins in the teaching of Zarathustra, had not managed to hold all their adherents in the face of the persuasive approach of the Christian gospel.

6. The revenues of the missionary societies had shown a steady increase. The amounts contributed were still minimal as compared with the sums which Christian congregations thought it necessary to spend on improving their own amenities. But the penury in which the great pioneers had subsisted was now a thing of the past, and it was possible for missions to launch out on enterprises educational, medical and social, such as could not have been dreamed of in earlier days.

7. Mott had seen the great universities of the Protestant world drawn into the missionary enterprise in a way that would not have been thought possible in his own undergraduate days. Many of the great missionaries of the earlier days, such as Robert Moffat and his son-in-law David Livingstone had been drawn from the class which in those days was known as 'the respectable poor'. Few of the missionaries from the continent of Europe had received a university education. Now, as a result of the religious revival which had been sweeping through the universities, owing mainly to the work of men like Mott himself, men and women of the highest intellectual calibre and drawn from the 'upper classes' were making themselves available in considerable numbers for missionary work in every part of the world.

8. The churches were beginning, though in many cases only just beginning, to recognize expansion into the non-Christian world as a natural part of the life of a church. Opposition to every form of missionary work was still strong, even among those who professed the Christian faith, but it was less vocal than it had been in earlier times. The change was in part due to the work of J. H. Oldham, secretary of the Edinburgh Conference, who had had the hardihood to invite no less a person than Randall Davidson, Archbishop of Canterbury, to be present and to address the Assembly. The presence of that great prelate was in itself sufficient to ensure that the missionary enterprise could no longer be dismissed as the concern only of a group of hot-headed enthusiasts.

9. Signs of Christian co-operation were beginning to make themselves manifest on a scale never seen since the Reformation. From 1855 onwards missionaries of many different groups in India had been meeting from time to time to confer and to share experiences. The Madras Conference of 1900, the first to be carefully planned and prepared for, had already pointed the way to the fuller achievements of Edinburgh 1910. As a result of such co-operation, the principle of comity, peaceful co-existence without mutual aggression and rivalry, had come to be accepted as the norm by the majority of missionary organizations.

10. Most important of all, the missionary overseas no longer found himself isolated in his efforts. He was increasingly sur-

rounded and supported by colleagues drawn from among the peoples whom he had come to win for Christ. Edinburgh 1910 was a missionary conference, and of the seventeen or eighteen members from the 'mission fields' the majority had come by special invitation from the central organization of the Conference, and not as representatives of overseas churches. But the more prophetic spirits in the Edinburgh meeting had already become aware of the shift in emphasis; the mission had begun to be seen as the temporary phenomenon, destined to be replaced by the permanent reality, the Church.

All these factors in the situation were verifiable and solid realities. It was natural that the Conference should give thanks that so much more had been achieved than had been thought possible by Carey and his friends. Had not Robert Morrison of China limited his hopes to the view that at the end of fifty years of labour there might be in existence a Chinese church with perhaps a hundred members; what would he have said if he could have known of the thousands for whom the spokesman in Edinburgh was Cheng Ching-yi? It was equally natural to suppose that the curve of prosperity would continue to rise, and that a great period of missions would be followed by even greater days. There were, however, not lacking in the Assembly observers of the signs of the times, who had noticed dark clouds banking up in what seemed to others to be still bright and hopeful sky.

2. Darkening Horizons

In 1905 Japan had entered into war with Russia, and for the first time since the recession of Turkish power two centuries before, an Asian nation had inflicted decisive defeat on a western power.

The event seems to have had surprisingly little effect on the thinking of western nations and western churches. The Japanese had in an astonishing way modernized themselves by the enthusiastic adoption of western culture and technology. By making a treaty with Britain in 1903 they had secured admission to the exclusive western club, whereas the west had always suffered from an uneasy uncertainty as to whether Russia was or was not really a part of Europe. But a cursory survey of the

Indian press at the time of the Japanese victory will suffice to reveal how differently the event was regarded throughout the eastern world. The west was seen to be no longer unassailable. In all those countries in which the colonial yoke was beginning to feel grievous, men began to hope for another world revolution in which the west would find its proper place, alongside of (but no longer in a position of artificial superiority to) the much more ancient civilizations of Asia.

This was only the beginning of change; far worse was to follow. In 1914 Europe was plunged into the first of those insensate civil wars in which it ruined itself financially and threw away to no advantage the dominant position in the world which had been built up by centuries of patient effort. From the Christian point of view the most serious consequence of the war was that the idea of the Christian west, which had never had substantial reality, simply vanished into thin air. Up to 1914 it had been possible to claim that certain forms of undeniable progress – in the administration of justice, in the sharing of power through democratic process, in the emancipation of women and in wider educational opportunity – had been the consequence of the application of Christian principle to social and political life. But what was Christian principle? The four years of war convinced the world outside Europe that the claims made on its behalf were hypocritical, and that in time of crisis the nations of the so-called Christian world would make their decisions, just like other nations, purely in terms of self-interest and without reference to any other principles whatsoever.

In February 1917 western Europe became aware that a revolution had taken place in Russia. Only very gradually did the full significance of these events penetrate the consciousness of the world outside the regions immediately affected. In Britain many were prepared to welcome the revolution . . . believing government in Russia to be so bad and oppressive that change of any kind could only be for the better. Indeed, in the early days it seemed that the revolution would move in a democratic direction, and that constitutional reforms would bring Russia nearer to those nations which, according to their own understanding of the situation, were fighting on behalf of human dignity and freedom. The shadow of Lenin had not yet fallen athwart the world.

Few single events have so deeply influenced the history of the world as the action of Germany in sending Lenin with a few of his companions in a sealed train from Switzerland to a Russia already deep in the throes of revolution. Even after the arrival of the exiles in their own country, it was by no means certain that the Bolsheviks would be able to seize power and to direct the revolution on strictly Marxist lines. Only a combination of luck and ruthlessness put power into their hands, and gave Lenin the chance to fashion a new world according to his own ideas.

In 1917 the nature of Marxism was little understood in the English-speaking world. The nineteenth century had believed in human progress. Under the influence of the liberal dream and a misapplication of Darwinian ideas of evolution it was taken for granted that progress could be only towards greater democratic freedom, broadening down from precedent to precedent. Man had at least a measure of liberty to determine his own future, and democracy was based on the idea of individual responsibility. Now the world was confronted with a system claiming to be scientific, indeed to be the only true science of man in society, in which only limited space was left for freedom, since everything would evolve according to a predestined pattern, determined by the very nature of things, which it was beyond the power of any man to alter. The revolution was the great reality; those who refused to accept it must simply be swept away. In the new order there was to be no place for religion, since all that was simply 'ideology' in the Marxist sense of that word, the invention of the possessing class to sanctify its aggressions by branding with the infamy of sacrilege any attempt on the part of the oppressed to assert themselves by rising against the oppressors. Persecution of the Church was justified in the early days of the revolution on the ground of too close an association of that Church with the authority which was to be destroyed. Later, though full freedom was given for anti-god campaigns, persecution was felt to be unnecessary, since religion, having no roots in reality, would soon wither away and disappear.

The full significance of all this only gradually dawned on the rest of the world. Nations, like individuals, are determined almost as much by 'the Other' as by what they themselves are. What claimed to be the free world now found itself opposed by a permanent Other, an alternative view of man and of the future of man in the world. Every axiom of western thinking was to be continuously challenged. Grounds might be found on which the western concept of liberty could be defended; it could never again be taken for granted. The Christian Church in all its various forms had grown up as an integral part of the western world; it could not but feel itself threatened in the threats directed against western political organizations.

The Marxist attacks on religion in general and on the Christian faith in particular were the most obvious factor in the new situation faced by the Church after 1917. But the Marxist was not alone in his hostility to religion. The ferocious attacks on the Christian faith (by which the second half of the nineteenth century had been marked) continued, though in rather different forms.

Many of the most influential philosophers in the English-speaking world could find no place at all for religion. Bertrand Russell was perhaps the most widely-read thinker in the period with which we are dealing. He took a limited view of the possibilities of human knowledge, and did not think that man's capacities are such as to give him any reliable evidence of existence beyond the range of those existents which can be the objects of scientific observation and research. Towards the end of his life he seemed to show signs, in the ideals to which he gave his allegiance, of a return in the direction of his evangelical upbringing; but he seemed never to go beyond an almost rueful recognition that there might be realities undreamed of in his earlier philosophy.

The title of Sigmund Freud's well-known book *The Future of an Illusion* (Hogarth Press) indicates in a single, well-chosen phrase the nature of his attack on religion. Freud was not concerned to deny the existence of religion as a human phenomenon; he encountered it in the minds of the patients he treated. He did emphatically deny that there was any external reality corresponding to what he observed in the human mind; all was due to projection outwards from the human consciousness, and objective reality was not to be looked for in religion. It is clear that at this point Freud was going beyond his competence as a psychoanalyst. The question of the relationship between external realities and human consciousness belongs to the realm of philosophy, and on such issues Freud was singularly ill equipped to pronounce. But his words carried weight, especially in the United States, even among those who had not read his writings,

8

and the idea that religion is mere illusion proved especially attractive to those who were already anxious to rid themselves of the burden of that illusion.

Hard on the heels of the psychologist came the linguistic analysts. In his now famous book *Language, Truth and Logic* (Victor Gollancz, 1936) Professor A. J. Ayer put forward the view that all metaphysical and religious statements are simply nonsensical. To say that God exists is meaningless; to say that he does not exist is equally meaningless. There is no point in asking whether the statement that God is love is true or not; the fact is that no meaning at all can be attached to these words, which are therefore noises without significance, or sheer nonsense. This radical view was defended on the basis of what came to be known as the Verifiability Principle, sometimes stated in the form that the meaning of a proposition is the method of its verification. But since there is no known method by which such a statement as 'God is love' can be empirically verified, it must be dismissed as not being a fit subject for rational discourse. The linguistic analysts have to some extent departed from the extreme position from which they started, and are prepared in a measure to recognize the significance of symbolic or analogical utterance. But it has not proved easy for those without extensive training in philosophy to spot the fallacies in their arguments and to believe that the expression of Christian faith may have both meaning and relevance.

In the nineteenth century missionaries had entertained a sanguine belief that, under the impact of the gospel and western science,[1] the ancient religions would quietly collapse and leave a vacuum into which Christianity would triumphantly enter.

There were grounds for this optimism which, as far as the first part of the statement was concerned, was shared by sceptics who would gladly have seen the disappearance of every form of religion. But the expected did not happen. The ancient religions have rallied their forces and are in better heart than they were when the first shock of the Christian impact struck them a hundred-and-fifty years ago.

During half a century adherents of these religions did suffer

[1] The collocation is interesting. It is clear that the missionaries of that date regarded religion and science as allies and were unaware (or refused to consider the possibility) of a clash and conflict between them.

from a certain sense of inferiority. For centuries they had lived in ignorance of everything outside their own restricted world. Their great days of inspiration lay far in the past, and they had tended to become content with the mere repetition of formulae and with ceremonies which no longer had relevance to the present. The west burst in upon them with all the prestige of invention, enterprise and military power. The latter seemed to have no more than limited power with which to oppose the invasion.

A turning-point was reached in 1893, the year in which the World's Parliament of Religions was held in Chicago. The ancient religions made audible their claim to be received as on an equality with the newer religions of the west; they could safely leave to the west pre-eminence in the world of mere technology, and rest their claim on the ripe spiritual wisdom that had distilled through many centuries. This point of view was persuasively put forward by the eloquent young Bengali who had taken the name Swami Vivekananda. There should be no question, he affirmed, of conversion from one religion to another. In order to become a Hindu a Christian need not cease to be a Christian, since all religions are essentially one. Let us learn to live together in peace and mutual harmony. The Swami did not trouble to conceal in private his contempt for the west, and its childish ignorance of all true spiritual reality. But his words carried weight. The American press loudly proclaimed its astonishment at the arrogance of the churches in sending missionaries to Asia, when it would far better become westerners to sit at the feet of Asians, who (it was clear) had much to communicate to the west of an inner wisdom of which it had been almost wholly unaware.

Swami Vivekananda claimed for Hinduism equality with the Christian gospel as a way to God. Thirty years passed by. Then each of the four great non-Christian systems – Hinduism, Buddhism, Islam and Marxism – was claiming superiority to Christianity on the grounds of superior age, deeper philosophy, practical worth, or scientific excellence. Christianity was quietly moved from the top to the bottom in the scale of religious values. And there were some in the west who were ready to applaud this dethronement of what had come to be regarded as a western religion, and to hail as liberation the renaissance of the ancient faiths of the east.

These voices had by now become somewhat clamorous. To

them were added the dulcet tones of the cultural anthropologist. The nineteenth century had indulged in wide-reaching theories as to the origins and nature of religion. These had now given place to much more accurate knowledge of the beliefs and practices of many races based on accurate field-work. Each religion was seen in relation to the culture of its adherents; indeed some investigators had come to regard religion simply as one aspect of culture. Many followed Emile Durkheim in this social interpretation of religion. Religion is the cement by which each particular society is held together in unity, the myth invented by each society, in which it saw itself, its own being, unified and glorified.[2] On this view religion is seen as something essential to the life of a society. Nothing, therefore, could be more harmful than the attempt to replace one set of myths with another. Within limits, the Christian myth has proved itself (on this view) appropriate to the world of western culture. The efforts of the Christian missionary to impose that myth on other cultures with which it has no relationship can only be destructive of the life of peoples exposed to such irrational cultural aggression.

Assaults from without have been contemporaneous with a certain diminution of Christian substance from within. The religious understanding of man and his place in the universe has been superseded in the minds of many by a secularist view, in which no place is accorded to values other than the purely material, and in which the horizon is narrowed down to include only such things as can be measured, numbered and weighed. Many teachers have absorbed this view and have passed on to their pupils the conviction that 'the scientific method is the only dependable method of attaining truth in every field, and that all other methods produce mere opinions which cannot be verified by others and are therefore worthless'. In consequence the spectrum of the human mind has been tragically narrowed to exclude the high and the holy. 'Many in our scientific age find it

---

[2] Durkheim's great work *Les Formes Elémentaires de la Vie Religieuse* appeared in 1912 (Eng. trans. Allen & Unwin, 1915). Unfortunately Durkheim had accepted the view that totemism, a supposedly universal phenomenon, was the source and origin of every religion. Later investigation has shown this assumption to be at best highly questionable. Nevertheless there is much in Durkheim's work which is highly valuable, and his views continue to be influential among students of religion.

difficult to accept religious beliefs and . . . some find the religious language used in church and synagogue completely meaningless. This causes them to dismiss man's religious experience as merely "subjective", and the beliefs that have arisen from it as only "projections of the imagination reflecting the childish beliefs of a pre-scientific age"' (George F. Thomas, *Philosophy and Religious Belief*, Charles Scribner's Sons, 1970, p. ix).

It is hardly surprising that, under the combined pressure of so many attacks, some Christians began to despair of the republic. Some came to regard the institutional church with anger and disdain. Has the church done anything other than fossilize the prejudices of past ages? Has it not so closely identified itself with the establishment as to have lost all capacity for prophetic insight and witness? Are we not more likely to encounter the living Christ outside the church than within it?

Some have been inclined to despair of the gospel itself. The apparently negative results of the critical work of Rudolf Bultmann and others of his school have filtered down through the media to the consciousness of those who have had no theological training, and have raised doubts as to whether we know enough of Jesus of Nazareth to form the basis for any kind of gospel. Is salvation, whether of yesterday, or today, or tomorrow, more than a vocable which may once have had some meaning, but no longer rings any bells in the mind of the hearer?

If this were the whole picture, the prospects of the Christian faith in the world might well seem dark indeed. It was, however the case that some Christians managed to look out on this stormy scene with tranquillity, not hiding their heads in the sand or pretending that things are other than they are, but resting on a deep assurance that the Lord of history does not make mistakes, and that, as in the days of the prophets of Israel, through most discouraging circumstances his purpose is going forward to its appointed end. Christian confidence was not dead.

3. The Century of Achievement

Dr. John R. Mott lived to a great age, passing to his rest in 1954. If he had lived on six more years and had been able to celebrate in 1960 the jubilee of the Edinburgh Conference of 1910, how would he have looked back on the half-century that

12

had passed over the world? Mott was a man of unquenchable optimism. To him difficulties always spelled opportunities, and disasters always gave assurance that God was about to do something new and spectacular in the history of the Church. If he could not always find God in the sunshine, he would find him in the shadows. His sources of information were always excellent and he knew much about the set-backs which have been recorded in our preceding section. Yet, knowing all that he knew, he might still have concluded that the optimism of 1910 was no idle dream but a recognition that the plan of God was still going forward in a perplexing world.

Professor K. S. Latourette, in his great *History of the Expansion of Christianity*, gave to the nineteenth century the title *The Great Century* (vols. 4 to 6, Paternoster Press). Looking back from the heights of 1975, we may feel inclined to agree that the nineteenth century was the great century of adventure, but to add that the twentieth has been so far the century of achievement:

1. The number of 'foreign' missionaries has at least trebled itself in the period now under review. The increase in the number of fully-qualified indigenous colleagues had been far more rapid. In some areas the number of ordained pastors of the local churches was in 1960 ten times what it had been in 1910.

2. Only after 1910 did the number of Christians in the non-Christian countries begin to expand with great rapidity. This is less true of Asia than of other parts of the world. Yet a careful study of the Indian census of 1961 has shown that, in spite of added difficulties arising from the political independence of India, the percentage of Christians in relation to the general population of the country had continued to increase in the previous ten years.

3. The Church has continued to press forward into the remotest and least promising areas of the world's surface. In 1952 Nepal, so long a country closed to every form of missionary enterprise, was opened (with some restrictions) to Christian work. By 1960 all the Eskimos in the frozen north of Canada were Christians and the first ordinations of Eskimos had taken place. The most inaccessible valleys of West Irian, the western

and Indonesian section of the great island known to the west as New Guinea, have been penetrated. With each year that has passed the lines of Bishop Heber's famous hymn

> Till each remotest nation
> Has heard Messiah's name

have become less of a vision and more of an experienced reality.

4   The influence of the gospel has penetrated far beyond the limits of the visible churches. In India there is hardly a city of any considerable size that does not have its *Christu Jayanti*, its festival of the birth of Christ, at which leaders of the most varied religious communities are not hesitant to stand up and bear witness to what they have learned from one whom they are prepared today to salute as one of the saviours of mankind. The legal abolition of untouchability has been one of the great achievements of independent India. It may be said that legal enactment has not yet made much difference in the villages of India; but the Act was a step in the right direction. It is unlikely that it would have been passed, had the way not been prepared by the ceaseless protests of missionaries against injustice, and the change in the climate of public opinion which had been brought about through familiarity with the Christian gospel.

5. In 1910, Christian co-operation was still in its initial stages. The International Missionary Council did not come into being until 1921. By 1960 almost every country of the west had its national missionary conference. Almost every country in the third world had its council, through which the efforts of innumerable missionary societies and local churches were co-ordinated. Co-operation with Roman Catholics, regarded by many in 1910 as unthinkable, has become a self-evident reality in many parts of the world. All this is taken so much for granted today that those who look back on history cannot but wonder that the missionary enterprise ever managed to make progress without such aids.

6. In 1910 the maturity and independence of the third world churches was a new and unfamiliar subject. By 1960 the stability of these churches had been tested in a multitude of ways. During the second world war the Battak church in Sumatra had been left for a considerable period without any foreign help at all. It

14

emerged from its harsh testing under years of Japanese domination stronger than it had been before it had entered into the ordeal, and with a firm determination to take into its own hands its future and its destiny.

7. The distinction between sending and receiving churches was beginning to lose its validity. The Church of South India (formed in 1947) is still glad to receive help from overseas. But it has for a number of years maintained its own missionaries in Papua and later in Thailand. A remarkable lay movement has come into existence within that Church with the object of sending out Christian witnesses to parts of India which are almost as foreign to the South Indian as India is to the European or American.

It is never easy to determine at any particular moment whether the cause of Christ in the world is advancing or falling back. Any general statement is likely to be so general as to be misleading rather than enlightening. It may be more profitable first to consider separately a number of regions, and only after that has been done to arrive at certain tentative conclusions:

1. In communist-controlled countries, even where persecution of religion is not the order of the day, the churches are passing through difficult times which show no signs of coming to an end. Yet to the surprise of the committed Marxist, religion has refused to follow what ought to have been the natural course of events and just to lie down and die. There are signs that the younger generation in Russia is rediscovering with interest the Christian past of the nation, and that young people are beginning again to appear in the churches.

No reliable information has been received for years as to the number of practising Christians in China, but it is clear that the Church still exists. Inhabitants of the Central Kingdom always assume that everything Chinese is better than anything in the rest of the world. It is unlikely that Chinese Christians are in this respect different from their brethren of other persuasions. They are almost certainly of the opinion that they are the only true Christians left in the world, all others having yielded to the blandishments of the capitalist caricature of civilization, and that the time will come when it will be possible for the Chinese remnant to sally forth to the reconversion of degenerate Christendom.

2. In the rest of eastern and southern Asia the Church seems to be engaged in a holding operation, not losing ground but not gaining rapidly. This is not surprising in a period which has seen grave political unrest in South Korea, the wars which have brought into being the new country called Bangladesh, and in many countries anti-Christian prejudices accompanying the attainment of political independence. The exception to this generalization appears to be Indonesia, the scene of some of the most remarkable movements in the Christian world today. It is not easy to get full information about these movements. The prudent Indonesians prefer not to advertise them too extensively, not wishing to make of themselves a kind of eighth wonder of the world.

3. The Middle East is so rent by the feuds between Israel and the Arab world as not to offer favourable ground for the Christian mission. Yet the churches are holding on and, in some countries such as Iran, are slowly growing. The success of the World Council of Churches in holding a meeting of Muslims and others with Christians in Beirut (March 1970) indicates a certain loosening of the tension between Muslim and Christian which may be full of promise for the future.

4. Of Europe west of the iron curtain there is little that is encouraging to say. Church attendance continues to decline. Questionnaires and opinion polls show a general opinion that the churches no longer play an important part in national life and in the places where decisions are made that affect the lives of many people. Yet it is evident that there is still a deep though confused interest in religion, and that clear, positive presentation of an intelligible gospel is listened to with attention, though not always with agreement.[3]

5. The peak of the prosperity of the North American churches seems to have been reached in 1960 or about that time. Now the American churches have to run faster in order to remain where they are. Scepticism has made deep inroads into the field of faith. Yet the American people is at the present time in an immensely serious and reflective mood. The successive revelations of the Watergate affair have caused many to ask whether the phrase 'a

[3] In a recent opinion-probe in England, nearly two-thirds of those questioned returned the surprising answer that they used some form of prayer every day.

16

nation under God' really has any meaning at all, and whether the recovery of meaning might not be advantageous. The immense sales, recently recorded in the *Christian Century*, of every existing translation of the Bible, especially of such modern paraphrases as *Good News for Modern Man* and *The Living Bible*, make it plain that literally millions of Americans have the feeling that the Bible still has something to say to them, though they may have very little idea of what its message is.

6. Latin America is today a continent of hope, or perhaps it would be truer to say of mingled hope and despair. Hopes of political reform have to a large extent been frustrated. But the progress of the Evangelical Churches (Latin Americans prefer not to use the term 'Protestant') continues to be astonishingly rapid, especially among those on the lowest income levels. This work is now carried on almost exclusively by Latin Americans and not by foreigners. At the same time the Roman Catholic Church is in process of creating for itself a new image. For a number of years Vatican policy was to put new life into the stagnant mass of a rather somnolent Church by pouring in large numbers of bishops and priests from abroad. This process still continues; but the Roman Catholic Church in Latin America is beginning to produce its own prophets, some of whom have been heard far beyond the limits of their own countries.

7. Africa is the second continent of hope. Political change has come about with almost incredible rapidity. Colonial control has vanished within the space of a dozen years and by the younger generation independence is taken as a matter of course – they have never really known anything else. In some areas, as in Zaïre, the confusion resulting from the achievement of political independence has not been favourable to Christian advance. But nothing seems able to check the steady and confident advance of the Christian churches. For all the inroads made by the materialism of the west, the African continues to be a religious being, and, of all the religions at present being offered to him, Christianity in one or other of its various forms seems to fit in best with the ideals that he has formed for himself. The intensely interesting phenomenon of the African Independent churches shows that the African, so far from regarding Christianity as the white man's religion, is now taking it as his own.

To sum up a complex picture in a few sentences is a difficult task. The Christian has no ground for the easy and complacent optimism which has sometimes ruled the thinking of his predecessors in the faith. But equally there is no need for gloomy prognostications of unending defeat. It is already clear that the prophecies of those who expected religion to pass away and to be replaced by science or scientific humanism were based on wishful thinking and not on observation of the facts. Religion is too deeply based in the needs of the human spirit to disappear so easily. Of the religions that claim universal significance Christianity is by far the most widely disseminated, and seems to have made the best adjustment to the new climate created by science and technological progress. There are at the moment no towering Christian figures of the eminence of William Temple or Karl Barth; but a great deal of ability is going into the task of Christian apologetics and exposition. Publishers are again finding it worthwhile to put religious books on the market in large quantities.

All this, however, does not add up to an affirmation that Christian progress will be automatic, continuous and easy. The approach of human beings to religious questions will become increasingly critical, as education becomes more widely available. The enquirer will ask for reasons, and if these are not given in fairly satisfactory form he is likely to turn elsewhere for answers to his questions. He will expect to experience religious life not as some excrescence only remotely connected with other aspects of his being, but as a reality at the heart of affairs and closely integrated with all other aspects of human life. The churches have hardly begun to work out what all this will mean for the work of the Christian evangelist.

4. Penitent Churches

The Church of Jesus Christ is today a world-wide Church. It remains, however, true that the great majority of Christians live in western countries, and are members of church bodies which have had a long and varied history. In other chapters of this book we shall have much to say about Christians' problems and achievements in other parts of the world. It may be useful to end this chapter by asking how these great and ancient churches see themselves today. What image of themselves have they been able to form in these days of crisis?

The most important fact about the churches of the western world today is that they are, almost without exception, penitent churches. They have learned to look at themselves with a critical and appraising eye, and these are some of the things that they have seen:

1. These churches have too long and too easily accepted as natural the disparity in wealth between east and west, or, as it should more accurately be expressed now that Japan has joined the wealthy nations of the world, between north and south. The churches cannot of themselves solve economic problems. They remain indifferent to them at peril of their lives.

2. The attitude of too many western Christians (and of those who have represented them abroad) towards peoples of other and 'inferior' cultures has all too often been one of patronizing superiority. The churches have at times joined with the trader and the government administrator in destroying what might well have been preserved, and in levelling out the rich and interesting differences between civilizations.

3. Western missions, like western nations, have from time to time broken up the unity which existed in a nation, a clan or a caste, and have not replaced it by any genuine unity in Christ.

4. Representatives of the west have often been insensitive to the needs and desires of those whom they have come to serve, and to the wounds inflicted on the spirits of proud and sensitive peoples; the latter have felt in the westerner a contemptuous disregard of the aspirations towards independence which they themselves have considered as no more than legitimate.

5. The extent to which Christian missions have been involved in the politics of the colonial powers has been much exaggerated; but there is a measure of justice in the complaint that the recognition of injustice has been more often followed by pious resolutions than by vigorous attempts to see that the injustices were rectified.

6. The west has suffered from the commercialization of religion. Even where the separation of Church and state has been most rigidly maintained, the churches have readily accepted benefits from the state in such matters as the exemption of church property from taxation, and have been in consequence

tempted to measure their own prosperity in financial terms, and to suppose that an extension of financial power will be accompanied by a corresponding development of spiritual strength.

7. The west, as is almost inevitable in countries with a long tradition of a partially Christianized civilization, has tended to suppose that its way of doing things is the only possible Christian way. This has led to failure to realize that there may be spiritual resources in other traditions on which the Church has yet to learn to draw, and that there may be valid forms of expression of the Christian faith widely different from anything that has become current in the west. This westernization of the Church has only in part been corrected by the recent developments of interest in the Orthodox Churches of the east – and viewed from Asia, even these churches are still western.

8. The churches have shown a remarkable capacity for adapting themselves to what are basically unchristian situations, and are therefore far more at home as part of the establishment than as unsparing critics of the establishment where it is at fault.

9. The churches no longer stone the prophets. They either paralyse them with flattery, or accept just so much of their teachings as will quieten potentially agitated consciences, and so make them even less sensitive to the need for radical change.

The list could be indefinitely prolonged. What is important to note is that these are criticisms directed by the Church against the Church, and not the loud cries of the enemies of the Church bent on its destruction. (The enemies do also utter loud cries. So do critics of the western churches from the third world, as has been all too painfully evident in the last World Assembly. But that is another story.) This self-criticism is the outward sign of an inner awareness which can accept criticism, whether directed from without or within, and transform it into the spirit of penitence.

Penitence must be understood in its proper and biblical sense. We are often told to repent of the sins of our ancestors. But this is impossible. We may regret the offences of others, we can repent only of what we ourselves have done and of what we are. Mere self-laceration arising from an unclear sense of guilt is at best an unprofitable pursuit and at worst can lead to paralysis of the will. Some have become so aware of the weaknesses of the

Church as to have concluded that there is nothing to be done but to come out of it and start all over again – with no guarantee that the new edifice will not show the same cracks and imperfections as the old. Others are prepared to remain within the Church in a state of perpetual lamentation over a state of affairs which it seems beyond the wit of either God or man to repair. Each of these attitudes is literally hopeless. The outcome of penitence (if it is related to the reality of spiritual challenge and to the regenerative power of God) is resolute, constructive and carefully-considered action.

What the nature of that action should be we shall endeavour to assess in the pages which follow.

2

DIALOGUE WITH MEN OF OTHER FAITHS

1. A Shrinking World

Mission used to be an affair of far horizons. The missionary was the man who disappeared into distant and unknown lands, to return after some years to hypnotize western congregations with tales of adventure amidst uncouth and possibly dangerous aborigines. If any member of those remote peoples did manage to make his way to the west, he was likely to be handed on from place to place as a remarkable and probably fragile curiosity. Now we are all so mixed up together that the situation is entirely different from what it was a century ago. Mission has been washed up on our shores, and we have been washed up on the shore of mission.

Australia provides an interesting illustration of the change. Until the second world war Australia had lived in almost total unawareness of south-east Asia. The greater part of the white population had not too distant links with the United Kingdom. Increasing rapidity of travel was bringing the United States up over the horizon, and the industrialization of Japan had made the Australian aware of a threat to his 'white Australia' policy. But the Commonwealth link was a major factor in Australian thinking. The second world war changed all that. What Europe was accustomed to call 'the Far East' has now become for Australia 'the Near North', a world of realities to which in the past far too little attention had been paid. The cession of West Irian to Indonesia by the Dutch has meant that for the first time in history Australia (with its still continuing responsibilities for Papua–New Guinea) found itself with a long land frontier in common with a non-European government. Up to 1948 few if any students from Thailand or Malaya had studied in an Australian university. Now students from Asian countries, with the exception of Red China of course, are numbered in their hundreds; and the Australian student with his Christian background is likely to find himself sitting in the classroom with students who may be Hindus, Muslims or Buddhists.

Contacts work in other directions also. More people from the west are living abroad than at any time in earlier history. It had been thought that the political emancipation of the third world countries would be followed by a rapid decline in the number of resident foreigners. Hardly anywhere has this actually taken place. Nairobi in Kenya still gives the impression of being largely a foreign city. The foreign element is much more international and much less purely British than it was. There are large numbers of Germans and Scandinavians engaged in 'projects' of one kind and another, and of course the omnipresent businessman from America and from Japan. Many of these foreigners spend only a limited period in the country of their temporary adoption, and move on when their 'project' is completed. In a number of countries, especially those which are Islamic, foreigners find access to the society around them extremely limited, and tend to live among their own kind, with few friends from the other community. The meeting place is likely to be no more intimate than the business office, or occasionally an international club, and subjects of discussion are limited to generalities, only rarely touching on matters which if freely discussed might cause offence on one side or other. Propinquity is very different from integration; to an astonishing extent communities live side by side and remain in almost complete ignorance of the ideas by which the life of others is directed and of the ideals in the light of which they live.

And yet it is almost impossible for the foreigner to live in a country other than his own without to some extent being affected by sights and sounds which at first strike him as exotic. It may be no more than the presence in his house of servants of the other race. In an Islamic country he will find that he is expected to work on Sunday, and that Friday is the day of rest. In India work will be interrupted by festivals, concerning the origin and purpose of which he will ask questions (unless he is extremely insensitive). He comes back to his own country to some extent another and a better-instructed man.

Mutual ignorance has a very long history in the interrelations of different parts of the world. In the Middle Ages crusaders and Muslims lived for two centuries in close touch with each other – nor were they always hostile; yet how little each succeeded in learning about the mind and thoughts of the other! Crusaders seem to have lived and died with the belief that Muslims were idolaters, blandly unaware that if a Muslim sees an idol his first instinct is to break it in pieces. The Muslim seems to have been equally unshaken in his belief that the Christian worships three gods. It is true that the first translation of the Koran into Latin was made in Spain in the twelfth century, but only as the crusading period was drawing to its end was it possible for Ramon Lull (1235–1315) to come forward with his noble ideas of a deep and sympathetic study of Islam. Only then could there be his commonsense recognition of the fact that you are not likely to be able to talk to another person with any hope of mutual comprehension unless you have some idea not merely of what he is thinking, but also of the way in which his mind works. We may account it as progress that the ideas of Ramon Lull have now found acceptance almost everywhere in the Christian world.

2. Getting to Know

Missionaries are constantly accused of having been so full of the message which they wished to deliver to the ignorant 'heathen' as to have had little time to remember (and little concern to reflect on) the possibility that the 'heathen' might have some ideas of his own, and that it might be worthwhile to understand those ideas before attempting to change them. Recent study has shown that such affirmations rest on mythology rather than on fact.

Some missionaries, of course, were ignorant and obtuse. But others accepted from the start the need for understanding, spent years in patient research, and left behind them works of irreplaceable value. There would, I think, be general agreement that H. A. Junod's *The Life of a South African Tribe* (1912) is the best book ever written on an African people, written at a time before that people had been deeply corrupted by the infiltration of western ways; and that R. H. Codrington, with his book *The Melanesians* (1891, now a Dover Publication) in which he expresses regret that he had had no more than twenty-four years in which to study the mind of those interesting peoples, was one of the founders of the then unformed science of ethnology. Many of these pioneer works of missionaries are being reproduced today not by the missionary societies but by the learned organizations; the missionaries had the advantage of associating with these peoples as they really were, and reflecting a situation which has passed away and can never be recovered.

This is only part of the story. In nineteenth-century India, converts of the calibre of Krishna Mohun Banerjea and Nehemiah Goreh set to work to expound the Hindu systems of thought, primarily in order to convince their brethren who were not yet Christian, but also with a view to opening up to their western friends the mysteries of a world in which it was impossible that they should ever feel perfectly at home.[1]

All this belongs to the past. Today there is no excuse for mutual ignorance. Every major religion in the world has been carefully studied. The sacred books of these religions have been translated, faithfully though not always elegantly, into all the main languages of the western world. Popular books abound, though these have to be used with care as being at times more popular than reliable. Western scholars have made notable contributions; these are now balanced by original writings as the adherents of the various religions make their voices heard and expound these religions as they understand and live them.

It must of course be recognized that the study of books is only dialogue at long range, useful if nothing else is to be had, but not to be compared with the actual confrontation in which adherents of different religions meet in an amicable and courteous spirit for the exchange of ideas and the enlargement of mutual understanding. It is true that proclamation is part of the job of a missionary; but it is unlikely to be highly effective unless supplemented by personal acquaintance and friendly discussion. This has been understood by missionaries from very early times. Indeed we may go back to the second century and recall the dialogue of Justin Martyr with Trypho the Jew, a work in which the charming courtesy represented on both sides is a happy reminder that relations between Christians and Jews have not always been as acrimonious as they became in the Middle Ages in the west.

The first Protestant missionary to India, Bartholomew Ziegenbalg (1706–19) wrote after some years of missionary labour polite letters to a number of leading Hindus in the neighbourhood of Tranquebar, asking them to state their

[1] On all this see the excellent study of Robin Boyd, *An Introduction to Indian Christian Theology* (CLS, 1969).

25

objections to the gospel as he had preached it. Several equally polite replies were received. The objections recorded were not so much to the doctrines or ethical principles of the gospel as to certain social practices which were believed to be inseparably associated with it. It was for this reason that a century earlier Robert de Nobili, wishing to make himself as far as possible a Brahman for the sake of the Brahmans, had given up all European customs (such as the wearing of leather sandals) which he had found offensive to his Hindu friends. Ziegenbalg's approach does not seem to have led to anything beyond courtesy; it showed at least the desire for better acquaintance, and a recognition that the other party in a dispute always has the right to be heard.

More than two centuries after Ziegenbalg a notable American evangelist took up his method and carried it a good deal further. Reputations fade quickly and it is probable that a number among the younger generation of Christians have never even heard the name of Eli Stanley Jones, who died in 1973 at the age of 88. Yet in his great days Jones was probably (second to C. F. Andrews alone) the best-known western Christian in the whole of India. Each year he would take three months' leave, to be spent in reading, study and the very careful preparation of five lectures on Christian themes. The remaining months would be spent criss-crossing India, with apparently inexhaustible energy, delivering his lectures in all the main cities of what was still united India. Indians love oratory. Stanley Jones was a highly skilled and eloquent speaker, who at the height of his powers could collect in any city an audience of four to five hundred educated Hindus and Muslims eager to listen to his words.

This was the area of proclamation. But the speaker was well aware that this was only half the battle. To make his work complete he must meet some at least of his hearers at much closer quarters, hear their side of the argument and be prepared to learn as well as to teach. Therefore, towards the end of each week of lecturing, he would arrange for a group of anything from sixteen to twenty-five members, drawn from all the religious confessions, to meet him for informal and unfettered discussion. Some of these meetings have been described in a book very popular at the time of its appearance, *Christ at the Round Table*. It was made clear from the start that the object of these discussions was not conversion, at least in any immediate sense of that term, but information and mutual enlightenment. Moreover the order of the day was not the delivery of technical lectures on the tenets of the various religions – such information could be gathered from a great variety of books – but the sharing of experience. What does it mean to be a Hindu or a Muslim today? What does the high-caste Hindu experience when each morning he greets the light of day in the immemorial salutation of the *Gayatri*? What does it mean to the pious Muslim to repeat five times a day in Arabic the noble phrases of the obligatory prayers?

It was not always easy to keep the participants within the prescribed limits of discourse. The Hindu was all too ready to launch out on a panegyric on Hindu mysticism. The Muslim might feel himself impelled to orate about the glories of the Holy Koran as the final and incomparable Word of God to man. Nor can it be said that the Christian was always blameless. On one occasion a British military officer, with the usual tongue-tied hesitancy of the British when called upon to speak on any matter of religion, had tried in halting and stumbling fashion to explain what it meant to him to live as a Christian in the difficult atmosphere of a regiment of the British army in India. The effort was evidently considerable. He was followed by a Christian pastor, who glibly trotted out all the familiar phrases which even the non-Christians present had probably heard a hundred times before; the temperature at once dropped to zero. On the whole, however, the rules were kept and a real exchange of thought and experience became possible.

From time to time there were sad confessions from those to whom religion had ceased to mean anything at all – the material world had driven out all the associations of the spiritual. One hearer at least was saddened to note again and again the poverty of that which the non-Christian friends could contribute in the way of personal experience of religion, as contrasted with the splendour of the traditions which they claimed to represent. Yet each of these Round Table Conferences was an experience to be treasured, an enrichment of understanding in relation to men of other faiths.[2]

[2] In those days 'men' did mean 'men only'. It was not usual for women to take part in such public discussions, and I cannot recall the presence of a woman at any of the Round Table Conferences which I attended.

The method of dialogue with men of other faiths is therefore not new. It has, however, been brought before the consciousness of the Christian world in a new way by the emphasis recently laid upon it as the only method by which a Christian can properly approach one who does not share his faith. It was extensively proclaimed at the World Council's Fourth Assembly held at Uppsala in 1968. It was one of the main subjects of discussion at the Bangkok Assembly of 1973. Though less fully discussed than had been expected at the recent Nairobi Assembly, it was throughout in the back of the minds of those who attended that Assembly. It therefore demands the careful attention of all those concerned about the task of Christian proclamation in the world.

There is no official ecumenical doctrine on the subject. But certain principles of dialogue would probably be generally accepted in ecumenical circles:

1. We live in a pluralistic world in which many religions exist, and have to learn to co-exist within limited areas. The only way to peace is for all to recognize the existence and the rights of all the rest. The United States have had to wrestle with this problem in connexion with the existence of Protestants, Roman Catholics and Jews (with the Orthodox emerging as the fourth power) and have come up with the solution that the interests of all are best served by the complete separation of Church and state; the state is to maintain resolute neutrality over against every form of religion, except in so far as the maintenance of public order may make necessary a certain amount of interference. This may be held out to all states as an example to be followed.

2. This plurality of religions is likely to continue into a future as extended as can be considered by the human mind. The nineteenth-century expectation of the rapid disappearance of the non-Christian religions was based on a number of misconceptions, and cannot be seriously entertained by anyone today.

3. All religions bear witness at least in some measure to the presence and activity of God. This used to be claimed only for the great historic religions. We now see that even the primal religions of Africa and such areas as the South Pacific are intricately woven textures, covering every aspect of the life of a

people, and giving assurance of the presence and activity of God in every part of that life. In the past history has been written in western categories only, and civilization has been identified simply and explicitly with western civilization. As a result western people have tended to limit the idea of divine revelation and claimed for Christianity a unique status as the one religion in which any gleam of divine truth can be discerned. Wider knowledge has made this claim untenable. After all, these other religions have sustained the inner life of millions of people over many centuries. Is it possible to affirm that God had no hand at all in all this, and that all these different religions are variant forms of error and nothing more?

4. The Christian who wishes to enter into dialogue with those of other faiths must resolutely put away from himself every thought of intellectual, religious or cultural superiority, as though dialogue was a one-way traffic in which communication of truth would be from his side alone. Such an attitude is a relic of the old western superiority complex, and makes impossible from the start any dialogue on terms of equality and mutual comprehension.

5. The Christian must put away firmly the idea that it is his business to 'bring Christ' to the non-Christian. It is part of Christian belief that God has reconciled the whole world to himself in Christ, and that since the resurrection Christ is everywhere present in the world that he has redeemed. The non-Christian is part of this redeemed world. Therefore Christ is already present in the other whom we meet. The Christian comes not to bring Christ but to find him, though he may also be privileged to bring more clearly into the consciousness of the other the Christ who is already in him.

6. The Christian must approach the interlocutor in the hope that he will gain more than he has to give. He should go in the expectation that the other has more of God than he has himself, and that he will end the encounter with his awareness of God amplified and enriched.

7. There must be no question of conversion from one faith to another. Each must be encouraged to go forward to the highest level of attainment possible for him on the path in which he has already set out. Conversion has undesirable

associations of social and emotional disruption and these are likely to be harmful rather than helpful to the development of true spiritual life.

Not all Christians will agree that this is a satisfactory presentation of the Christian approach to dialogue. Naturally, however, it has been enthusiastically welcomed by Hindus and others to whom the Christian claim to the possession of all truth and the demand for conversion have always been anathema. To them it appears that the Christian has at last climbed down from his high horse, has abandoned his affirmation of the uniqueness of his faith and has so made possible real religious discussion on terms of equality.

Every Christian will readily admit his need to learn the lesson of humility, a virtue without which no other virtue can exist and which Christians have always found particularly difficult to practice. But humility and regard for truth are equal, and equally essential aspects of Christian responsibility for witness to the faith.

We have first, as Christians, to face the question of the authority on which we act. Are there any standards which the Christian as Christian is bound to accept? If so, in what direction shall we turn to find the definition of these standards? In the past Christians have been agreed that the New Testament is authoritative. It is not clear that the advocates of dialogue in its modern form would give unqualified adherence to this view. The writer to the Ephesians, recalling to his readers what they had been in their pre-Christian existence, reminds them that they had been 'without hope and without God in the world' (Eph. 2:12). The word in the Greek is very strong: it is literally, 'You were atheists'. Of course the writer does not mean that his readers had had no knowledge of God at all; in fact the trouble was that they had too many gods rather than too few. Nor is he writing to barbarians and savages; his readers as non-Christians had had around them the splendours of the greatest artistic civilization the world had ever known, and a whole variety of religions of different types and levels from which to choose. And yet he affirms that what has come to them in Christ is so transcendent, so wholly different from every other kind of religion that it is hard to find any standard of commensurability between the old and the new. The difference between them is not in degree but in kind. It is not a case of converging lines which, if produced far enough, will meet at some point as yet undefined and undisclosed. It is not even a case of parallel lines which will 'meet' at infinity. This and that are so different that this can never be changed into that, and that can never lose itself in this. We are dealing with different things and not with different forms of the same thing.

No one has ever surpassed Paul in his appreciation of the greatness of God's achievement in the Old Testament and of the glory of being a Jew. But he had learned by experience that all the greatness of that past was something that he had to cast on one side, to treat as refuse, in order that he might gain the benefit of being in Christ (Phil. 3:7–11).

These and similar passages of the New Testament (if we take them seriously) warn us that we may enter into dialogue rather too light-heartedly and may be led unawares into mistaking similarities for identities, and so to disregarding differences in meaning. Respect for other religions demands that we should deal with them as they really are and as they are understood by those who adhere to them.

There is a further point to be considered. In the outline of dialogue as at present understood, have we in fact gone beyond the limits of what we have described as friendly discussion with a view to mutual illumination, and possibly co-operation for purposes universally agreed to be desirable? This is suggested by the words of Dr. M. M. Thomas, when Moderator of the Central Committee of the World Council of Churches, in his address to the Nairobi Assembly (see *Breaking Barriers: Nairobi 1975*, SPCK, 1976):

> Is it not legitimate to welcome a Christ-centred process of inter-religious and inter-cultural penetration through dialogue? . . . Acknowledging the common humanity given through Christ, can we not work with men of all religions and of no religion for a secular human culture and community, and even for a secular humanism open to insights from all religions and ideologies, evaluated in the light of and informed by the true manhood of Jesus Christ?

A good deal of elucidation as to the meaning of the terms used seems to be demanded by such a declaration; but the general drift is clear. The aim of friendly discussion is mutual illumination. The concern of dialogue is with truth. Each in its own field is desirable, indeed necessary. The more deeply we can be led into understanding by way of amicable discussion, the better it will be for our own soul's health. But it is wiser not to call by the same name things that are radically different. There is a dreadful seriousness about genuine dialogue; it is almost literally a matter of life and death, as mere discussion never can be.

3. The Nature of Dialogue

In the development of true dialogue a special place must be accorded to Plato, or, if he is a true recorder, to his master Socrates. Some readers of Plato have been blinded by the astonishing literary brilliance of his writing, and have failed to note what is essential in the dialogues. Behind the sparkling skill of the dialectic, the digressions, the myths, the continual coruscation of wit, there is always present a profound seriousness; the concern of Socrates is that truth should emerge, not necessarily truth as he himself has begun by conceiving it, but truth in its original and pristine beauty.

Once this has been grasped, it is easy to see why Socrates throughout the whole of his teaching career was engaged in ceaseless and truceless war against those who are commonly known as Sophists. These teachers, as we see them in the pages of Professor W. K. C. Guthrie's excellent study,[3] were a product of urbanization, of increasing commercial wealth and of the beginnings of Greek internationalism, as the parochial Hellene began to move out of the narrow confines of his city-state into a rather larger world. The Sophist was by birth a citizen of one city only, but he tended to regard himself as a citizen of the world. He would move from city to city and offer his wares for sale – an unpardonable offence in the eyes of Socrates. One of the principal articles in his stock-in-trade was sheer cleverness in the manipulation of words. The height of the rhetorician's skill is to make the worse appear the better reason, and so to persuade men against their better judgement. In the process, truth disappears or is relativized to the point of near disappearance.

The nature of the opposition which Socrates had to face explains the deadly seriousness of his approach and the occa-

[3] In Vol. III of his great *History of Greek Philosophy* (Cambridge University Press, 1972).

sional ferocity with which he would pursue an interlocutor down the paths of his own folly. His emphasis on semantics, the study of the exact meaning of words, may seem to us at times tedious (though the need for it is brought home to us daily in the process of ecumenical debate). Carelessness in the use of words leads to inexactitude of thought, and this is exactly what gives the Sophist his chance. He can make use of precisely this lack of clarity – and sometimes indolence – to confuse all issues and lead men under the hypnotic effects of his eloquence to accept conclusions which in their sober senses they would be bound to reject. So Socrates intervenes to prick the bubble of sophistic fantasy with the sharp needle of his irony and we are back once again where we started. Yet not exactly where we started, for the process of jungle-clearing has had more than a negative value. We may be more ready than we were for the emergence of the splendour of truth.

We do not need to look far to see the relevance of all this to the age in which we live. It is by no means clear to all our contemporaries that the search for truth is either possible or desirable.

In a number of the disciplines widely pursued in our universities the question of truth is never raised at all.

Descriptive anthropology studies the innumerable ways in which groups of human beings have agreed to organize their lives, and the religions which are increasingly seen to underlie all such forms of organization. The anthropologist may hold that some cultures are better than others in the sense that they better promote the survival of the human race, or even that they tend to a more highly developed type of humanity. But he claims (quite rightly) that he is not concerned with the problem of the existence of any ultimate reality, or with the possible relation in which any particular culture may stand to that reality, if indeed any such should exist.

The sociologist is concerned with the organization and behaviour of men in societies. He has noted that religion plays a part in such organizations, and therefore a special subject called the sociology of religion has been developed. But to the question, 'Do you regard any of the religions which you study as being true?' his answer is likely to be a stare of astonishment; no question could be more alien to his enquiries.

There is no such thing as absolute truth in history. The

number of questions that can be asked about any historical situation is literally unlimited and a selection (inevitably to some extent arbitrary) has to be made if history is to be written at all. The discovery of new evidence may at any time upset old ideas and dissipate old prejudices.

In the field of morals few would claim either perfect objectivity or the universal applicability of any moral standards for which validity is claimed. Long before 'situation ethics' had been invented, the old proverb 'circumstances alter cases' had drawn attention to the need for flexibility in the application of moral rules. The most that would be claimed by the majority of moralists today would be a relative and limited validity.

If views of this kind are held, and it is not admitted that there are any absolutes in the field of morals and religion or that there is any such thing as absolute truth outside the field of pure mathematics, then dialogue in the sense in which we have been understanding the term becomes impossible. Discussion, comparison of ideas, exchange of experiences, will continue to be interesting and useful. But this process is radically different from dialogue in the true and Socratic sense of the term. Dialogue thus understood becomes possible only if there is agreement that the term 'truth' in religion has a meaning, that religion is related to some objective and ultimate reality, and that, although that reality will certainly prove to be far greater than the human mind will ever be able to grasp in its totality, some apprehensions will validate themselves as true, inasmuch as they do not obscure any part of that reality which is accessible to the mind of man.

The Christian is committed to the view that Jesus Christ *is* the truth; to the view, that is, that in proportion as Jesus Christ is understood, man's understanding of himself and of the world in which he lives can be indefinitely extended in the light of the revelation which Jesus gives of God, and that there is no fact and no circumstance which intrinsically falls outside that field of explanation. This does not involve the Christian in the claim that other religions bear no relation to the truth at all, still less in the claim that he himself has apprehended all the truth that is to be found in the Christ. But, as a believer, he does claim to stand in a particular relation to the truth as such, and not merely to 'his own truth' – whatever that phrase may be taken to mean.

Even if this understanding of the nature of Christian faith is accepted, it does not follow that every Christian is qualified either by knowledge or by temperament for the difficult task of dialogue with men of other faiths. Certain qualities may be required and certain rules may have to be observed if any profit is to result from the experiment. A tentative list of qualities and rules may be drawn up:

1. Courtesy is the first and most inflexible rule, if true dialogue is to be possible. A considerable measure of intensity of feeling may be generated if convictions are strong on both sides, and at certain points intractable contradiction cannot be avoided. But the moment courtesy goes out of the window, genuine dialogue goes with it.

2. There must be willingness to listen with patience, even if at times the interlocutor becomes prolix and the arguments adduced by him seem to be irrelevant. Not everyone is capable of stating a case succinctly, and few indeed are those who can keep their minds fixed for more than a few moments on the development of an argument.

3. There must always be deep respect for the personality of the partner in dialogue. His arguments may appear to be perverse and his attitude unyielding; but after all he has lived long in the light of the views that he is trying to express; any attempt to bring any kind of pressure on him to change those views will be self-defeating.

4. Each partner must be concerned to see the best in the point of view sustained by the other. In the past, Christians have been all too ready to contrast the best in Christianity with the weakest in Hinduism. They cannot complain if Hindu tactics today are to contrast the strengths of Hinduism with the weaknesses of the Christian world. But nothing is to be gained by either of these two approaches.

5. The Christian must never attempt to score a point by a slick or specious argument, or to bear the other down by the weight of superior knowledge or of superior skill in dialectics. Such action may lead to a kind of success, but it is much more likely to produce resentment in the one who feels that he has been unfairly scored off. All too often the victor in such a contest has to admit ruefully: 'I won my argument but I lost my man.'

6. Each partner must be prepared generously to recognize points scored by the other. In any debate it is most unlikely that all the scoring will be on one side. Unless each is prepared frankly to admit weaknesses uncovered in the case that he is presenting, the honesty of dialogue is impugned.

7. The aim of dialogue is decision. But decision must be carried out in absolute freedom by one who has freely reached the point of conviction. If decision has been in any way imposed by *force majeure* on the part of one side or the other, the rules have been infringed and the very purpose of dialogue has been frustrated.

Many Christians would not be prepared to enter into dialogue on the basis of such stringent rules as have here been set down.

One group would maintain that the task laid upon the Christian is to proclaim the gospel and nothing else. It may be that such an earnest Christian has not enquired into the possibilities for forthright proclamation in a Muslim country such as Somalia, where any expression that can be taken as derogatory to the dignity of the Prophet of Islam may render the speaker liable to prosecution for a criminal offence, or at best to deportation from the country.

Others may feel that even to suggest that there may be truth in other forms of religion from which the Christian should be glad to learn is in itself a betrayal of the incomparable truth of the Christian faith.

Yet others will feel that some dishonesty is involved if the Christian who is sure of the truth of the Christian faith is prepared as it were to put that conviction for the time being in cold storage and so to meet on equal terms those who are equally firm in maintaining the truth of their own position. It has to be admitted that the position of the Christian is in a certain sense dialectical. He is willing deliberately to make himself vulnerable. He has to hold simultaneously to the validity of his own conviction concerning the truth and to the recognition that he may not have all the truth and must be prepared to abandon anything that does not stand the test of strict examination and probing by others. This is no easy task. Dialogue is not for Christians who are not prepared to descend into the arena, as their Master did, unprivileged and unprotected. The partner in dialogue is always to some extent at risk; if he is not prepared to accept the risk, it will be as well for him to find some other form of activity.

4. Honesty and Decision

There is a limit, even in dialogue, to compliance and complaisance. We have said that the aim of dialogue is the emergence of truth. In so far as the Christian is convinced that Jesus Christ is the truth, that all secondary and partial truth is in some way related to him and that nothing which does not belong to the truth can survive in his presence, he is not called upon (as a condition for entering upon dialogue) to surrender any of these concerns. I am indeed concerned that Christ as the truth should appear, and should be seen to be the truth. But what my partner sees must be his Christ and not mine, his discovery and not my imposition upon him of my own limited and partial vision. Even as committed Christians, as we go forward in the Christian life, we are from time to time humiliated to discover how little we have really known of our Master. So if, when Christ appears, my partner sees in him things that I have never apprehended, and beholds a Christ in many ways different from the Christ to whom I have given my allegiance, this should be a cause for rejoicing rather than for dismay. It has always been our hope that, when the Hindu and the Buddhist turn to Christ, they will convey to us indispensable help in tracing out what Paul so sensibly calls the 'unsearchable riches of Christ' (Eph. 3:8). If his Christ differs in some ways from mine, that should be taken as evidence not of some subtle heresy, but of the authenticity of his vision.

These considerations will guide us as we consider the question whether conversion (in any sense of that term) is involved in dialogue, when the latter is pushed to the extreme limit of sincerity. Already some Hindus are saying, 'We really preferred the old missionaries. We knew they wanted to convert us, and we were on our guard. You say that you do not want to convert us; but we still think that you do.' Are they right? At all costs, we must be honest with ourselves and with them.

Many Christians in India today frequently use the following expression: 'It is our business to bring people to Christ, but not to make them Christians.' Once again, semantic work is called for. If this means simply that we are not to attempt to catch birds and to shut them up in the cages of our own particular denomination, that we are not to take hold of Hindus or Muslims and attempt to mould them exactly to some pattern which we have already formed in our own minds, there is not likely to be much disagreement with the sentiment. But more questions will inevitably arise than are covered by this all too easy answer.

If I take my partner in dialogue seriously, I cannot wish for him anything less than I wish for myself. What I desire for myself is that Christ should be all in all to me, that he should reign unconditionally supreme over every thought and word and deed, that my going out and my coming in should be ordered by his Spirit, and that he should be glorified in my body whether it be by life or by death. This is the surrender to which I desire that my interlocutor also should come. But is this not what is meant by being a Christian? If my friend comes to this point, is he not already a Christian, having repudiated every other lordship and accepted the exclusive dominion of One who will not permit any rival to himself in the heart of man?

What he does with this new allegiance, and what expression he gives to it, is his affair and not mine. No man has a right to demand of any other that he should be baptized, though he may point out to him passages in the New Testament dealing with this subject, and indicate that a decision one way or the other will sooner or later have to be reached. Since in so many communities the results of baptism are so momentous, indeed so disastrous, the nature of the decision must be determined by the one concerned and no one else.

At the present time a rather strong movement within the Christian church maintains the view that, where baptism is certain or likely to be followed by social ostracism and the total separation of the convert from family and friends and all earlier associations, he had far better remain an unbaptized believer, a friend of Jesus within a society which does not yet believe in him. Once baptized, he will lose every opportunity of witness to the people among whom he has lived. His act of apostasy – for such it will be deemed – will settle his friends in rigid hostility to a faith in which they might have begun to be interested. More over he may well find himself in a state of economic dependence on those who have brought about his conversion; history shows that this is a situation far from conducive to healthy, spiritual development.

38

Neither the problem nor the discussion is new. The question was ardently debated in India half a century ago. On the one side was Mr. Kandaswami Chettiar, a well-known member of Hindu society in Madras, who made no secret of his devout belief in Jesus Christ, but declared his intention of remaining in the Hindu society in which he had been born and in which he was living at the time. The tolerance practised within that society was such that no objection would be raised to his change of inner conviction or even to a certain measure of conformity to Christian practice, provided that he kept at the same time the essential requirements of membership in a Hindu family. But baptism is regarded by the Hindu, as it is by the Christian, as a kind of death. This would be the point of no return; if baptized, he would to all intents and purposes be dead to one world and have to find his unaccustomed way in another.

The contrary point of view was expressed by Mr. V. Chakkarai, a convert who had taken the fatal step of baptism. Mr. Chakkarai was well known as a harsh critic of all existing church bodies and in particular as an inveterate foe of missionaries; it was this that lent special weight to his words. He maintained that the idea that a Christian can continue to live as a member of a high-caste Hindu family is based on sheer illusion. The life of such a family is all of a piece. It is impossible to distinguish and to say, 'This is Hindu, but this is neutral'. Every part of the life of the family is shot through with Hindu thoughts and ideals; in such a situation it simply is not possible for a Christian to live without compromise.

The controversy will no doubt continue. It would be presumptuous on the part of one who has never been faced by the dilemma even to express an opinion. It must be left to those who have faced it to express their Christian judgement. Perhaps the best assessment of the situation ever written is that by Hassan Dehqani-Tafti, at the time of writing Anglican Bishop in Iran, in the account of his experiences in the book entitled *Design of my World* (World Christian Books, Lutterworth Press). Himself a convert from Islam, though not from Islam of a very fanatical character, he had to make up his mind on this question of baptism. The Christian believer reads in the gospels that Jesus bids his followers take up their cross and follow him. For a convert baptism certainly involves the taking up of a cross. But if the convert has reached the conclusion that this is a cross which the Lord himself is asking him to carry, what business has the Christian to stand in his way and advise him to act in disobedience to the inner conviction which he has reached by the exercise of his own independent judgement?

It has to be recorded as a matter of history that a great many of those who have come to believe in Jesus have felt themselves impelled (as was Mr. Chakkarai) to take the step of baptism. They seem to feel that what a man is inwardly he should also be outwardly. Perhaps even without having been thus instructed, they have come to understand instinctively that a Christian is not meant to stand alone. Knowing all that they do of the divisions, the weaknesses and the follies of the Christian churches, they yet run to the nearest Christian fellowship and demand to be admitted to its ranks.

5. Less Easy than might be Supposed

Those who advocate dialogue as the ideal method for meeting adherents of other religions seem to imagine that there will be no difficulty in finding partners prepared to enter upon dialogue on terms that will be acceptable to the Christian. In point of fact this is not nearly as easy as is often supposed.

It has often surprised me that Christians alone should be required to be tolerant in a world in which no one else is prepared to be tolerant. The dedicated Marxist regards himself as a man with a mission. He alone knows the truth about society and about the ways in which society changes; all other men walk blindly in the world of ideology. His sincerity demands that he should be a ferocious propagandist; the greater the sincerity, the greater the ferocity. The convinced Muslim is equally of the opinion that he has the whole truth, the final word of God to men, and that this truth must prevail over every other kind of truth, even over the truth as delivered by such eminent prophets as Moses and Jesus of Nazareth. To the Buddhist there is only one way, that proclaimed by Siddhartha, commonly called Gautama the Buddha. He alone was the Awakened One, when all other men were sunk in sleep; to call other men to awake is the task laid on the one who firmly believes himself to be in the Way, though he may know that he has not yet attained the goal. All these are propagandist religions and make no secret of it. A Christian cannot be regarded by them as anything other than conversion-fodder. The attitude of Jews and Hindus is naturally rather different; yet they too are not averse these days to drawing others into their folds.

Moreover we face the problem that few adherents of these other great religions have taken Christianity seriously enough to be interested in it or in the possibility of real dialogue with Christians. Whereas Christian scholars have written books of outstanding merit on religions other than their own, there has so far been no response from the other side. It is not possible to name one single book on Christianity by Hindu, Muslim, Buddhist, Sikh or Marxist, which can be compared in point of scientific weight and excellence with the best that has been written by Christian scholars on faiths other than their own. Certain studies have been made, but generally for controversial purposes. In consequence the writing tends to be superficial and at times to show sheer misunderstanding rather than apprehension of the significance of the faith allegedly under examination.

The fact is that the attitude of many of the leaders in the non-Christian world towards Christianity is so contemptuous that it is hard for them to consider that that faith might be a worthy subject of serious study.

The Hindu with his justifiable reverence for his own great tradition of wisdom in the Upanishads and the Hindu systems of philosophy is inclined to regard western philosophy as being on the whole a rather paltry affair, and to ask whether there is such a thing as a serious and consistent Christian philosophy.

The Buddhist, having long since excluded the idea of God, either as irrelevant to the business of redemption or as related only to lower levels of existence, is impatient when the Christian insists on raising the question of the existence and being of God. He has not generally shown himself friendly to the Christian view that the word 'God' means 'that than which nothing greater can be conceived', and that therefore when the Christian speaks of God he is moving in the same sphere as the Buddhist when he speaks of Nirvana, the ultimate reality.

The Muslim is committed to a greater respect for Christianity than either the Hindu or the Buddhist, since this is enjoined upon him by his own sacred book. But when a final and contemporary revelation has been given, why waste time in going back to an earlier doctrine which has been abrogated and superseded by that which has followed it, and which in any case was a religion intended by God only for Jews and blown up into a world religion only by the obtuseness and obstinacy of the early Christians?

The Christian is unlikely, therefore, to find immediately to hand the interlocutor who is qualified by knowledge, open-mindedness and readiness to serve as partner in dialogue in the sense in which we have defined it above. If he is fortunate enough to find such a partner, he is on his way to experiences of great subtlety and significance. The final result can be left in the hands of God. In the meantime he will find that his faith is:

. . . tested. He will be dealing with partners of penetrating intellect who will quickly detect any weak points in his position, and will demolish any argument which does not really establish what it sets out to prove.

. . . purified. He is likely to find that he has extended his line too far and is trying to defend positions that are really indefensible. Faith in its progress usually accumulates a good deal of superfluous luggage, accretions which have been there for a long time, but which in the light of strenuous criticism from outside are seen not to be necessary parts of that faith.

. . . modified. If dialogue in the sense in which we have defined it has really taken place, it is unlikely that the Christian participant will have learned nothing from his friends of other faiths. It is not so much that he will learn new things as that he will learn to look with new eyes on things that he already knows. From the Hindu for example he may learn how incorrigibly the west has come to identify reality with the visible and the tangible. St. Paul has taught us that the things that are seen are temporal, whereas the things that are not seen are eternal; this is a truth which Christians do not always succeed in bearing steadily in mind.

. . . strengthened. On what has his faith rested? If it has really been based on Jesus Christ, the Christian need have no fears as to the results of dialogue. It may well be that he has seen Jesus only very imperfectly and needs to learn from others to look at him again. But the more clearly Jesus is confronted with the greatest of the teachers of the other faiths – his teachings with their teachings – the more he is seen to tower above them all. It is not necessary to deny the greatness of Muhammad as prophet and leader of men to see that Jesus of

Nazareth is strong just where the prophet of Islam is weak. The *metta* – passionless benevolence of the Buddhist – is a noble concept; the *agape* – the love of God revealed in Jesus Christ – adds a dimension which to the Buddhist is unknown.

This then is the purpose of dialogue with men of other faiths: that truth may appear in all its majesty. The Christian is committed to the view that all truth, in whatsoever guise it may manifest itself, is from God. He is free to recognize truth which is not evidently and clearly related to the revelation of God in Jesus Christ; but he is not likely to give up his conviction that every such truth (in ways that we can see or in ways that we cannot see) is related to that supreme manifestation of the truth. In this sense, but in no other, the truths to be found in other religions may be seen as roads which lead, albeit circuitously and indirectly, to the one true God.

3

A MORATORIUM ON MISSIONARIES?

1. Missionary, Go Home!

In 1964 Dr. James A. Scherer, then Dean of the School of Missions of the Chicago Lutheran Seminary, wrote a book entitled *Missionary, Go Home!* Already at that time a number of leaders in the third-world churches were inclined to feel and to say that the day of the 'foreign' missionary was at an end; he had done well in starting the work of God in this or that area and in carrying it forward to a certain point, but now that his task had been accomplished, the time had come for him to bow himself gracefully off the stage and leave the work in other hands. What had been a kind of groundswell of opinion has become in more recent times an extremely vocal campaign, taking the form of a demand for a 'moratorium' on the services of all missionaries for a longer or shorter time, or for good and all. This term, for which in the sense commonly used in ecclesiastical circles there is no support in the English dictionary, seems to have become part of the ecumenical jargon with which we have to learn to live. 'Moratorium' was one of the subjects most prominently before the Assembly at Bangkok in 1973. It has been discussed in a large number of articles and reports.[1] Though it occupied less of the time of the Nairobi Assembly of 1975 than had been expected, it was much in the minds of a large number of those who attended that Assembly.

The case for the 'moratorium' is argued on many and diverse grounds. Perhaps four may be singled out as recurring in almost every statement on the subject:

1. The presence of the foreigner inhibits the ability of the third-world Christian to be himself and to develop the independence of thought and action without which a third-world church can never grow to maturity.

[1] A whole number of the *International Review of Mission* (WCC, April 1975) was devoted to this theme.

2. Financial aid from churches in the west hinders a church in growth towards self-support and produces an artificial estimate of the actual financial situation of such a church.

3. If even a single foreigner sits on a church board or committee, all the other members feel some unease and anxiety, and find it difficult to be their natural selves.

4. The foreigner (even when he does not intend it) is an obstacle in the way of the discovery of that identity which is one of the main concerns of third-world Christians, as they seek to find themselves in the new and uncertain world into which they have been introduced.

It must not be supposed that there is general agreement in these churches on the subject of the 'moratorium'. Bishop Festo Kivengere of Uganda, speaking at the Assembly in Lausanne in 1974, pointed out that the question had never been discussed at the 'grass roots' and that the opinions of a limited number of church leaders could not necessarily be taken as expressing the view of the churches as a whole. Churches in different areas and at different stages of development might be expected to come up with a whole variety of answers.

In a number of areas, what seems to lie behind the demand is the generation gap in rapidly changing situations, and the co-existence of three very different attitudes towards the presence of the foreigner in the Church. The generation of the first converts had little difficulty in adjusting to the presence of the foreigner. He was the man through whom the great deliverance had come. The greatness of the gift that he had brought carried with it respect for the one through whom the gift had come. There were two ladders of ascent in the Church. The indigenous Christian had his own ladder which he could climb to a position of leadership and influence among his own people. The missionary on his ladder dealt with a whole range of questions – relationships with a missionary society in the west, finance and so on, with which the new Christian was not very much concerned. There was in most cases little sense of rivalry, and the relationship was one of deep mutual respect and affection.

As the Church grew and developed, the question naturally arose as to why there should be two ladders. President Kaunda of Zambia has placed it on record that as a boy he wondered why the missionaries went about in cars, whereas his own revered father made his peregrinations on a bicycle. Why should certain offices be reserved exclusively for the foreigner? Why should limits be set to the level to which the indigenous Christian might hope to rise in a church which he was feeling increasingly to be his own? Inevitably, feelings of rivalry arose; the missionary came to appear as an obstacle to the Christian of the younger church in his attempt to become a fully responsible member and leader of the local church. Missionaries in some cases retaliated by a defence of their own position, which was at times based on a less than fully Christian understanding of the situation.

A yet younger generation views the matter through different eyes. These young people take political independence for granted; they have never known anything else, and earlier political struggles are to them simply a historical memory. They are fully used to international action in other spheres, whether it be the extinction of the mosquito by the World Health Organization, or the introduction of better strains of food-grains among the farmers by teams of expert agriculturalists. Why should the Church not also be international? This point of view is very clearly present among university students. What the student wants is to be well and thoroughly taught. If there is a national to do the job, he will be very pleased; if not, let the foreigner carry on until a national is ready to take over from him. A few years ago, it was recorded that the teaching staff of the University of Nigeria at Nsukka was drawn from twenty-two nations. Naturally the process of indigenization must go forward as rapidly as possible; but the example of many western universities in retaining an international character is one that is likely to be followed by universities in other parts of the world. And if by universities, why not by the Church, which after all is the most international society on the face of the earth?

There is a divergence of viewpoints within individual churches. There are also diversities of age and development as between the various churches in the third world.

Missions began to take hold in India more than a hundred years ago. Fifty years ago, the moratorium idea was rather strongly present in the Indian churches, though of course that particular word was not used. Now the tensions seem to have passed away. If Indian churches do not see the Indian who seems qualified to become their bishop, they have no hestiation in electing a foreigner, a proceeding to which the government of independent India seems to raise no objection at all. When the first Indian bishop of the Tamil Evangelical Lutheran Church in South India retired, the Christians decided that for the time being they needed a foreigner as his successor; all they sent to Sweden were the names of three Swedish missionaries; there the final decision had to be made. If any critic objects that this is regression to a colonial past, the Indian Christian is ready with his reply: 'You have recognized our full spiritual independence, have you not? If we exercise that independence by choosing the man whom the Holy Spirit seems to be pointing out as the one best qualified for the job, who are you to object to this exercise of our independence?'

In Africa most churches are a generation or two younger than those in India. It is here that the call for a moratorium is most loudly and clamorously expressed. Memories of a colonial past are still recent and in some cases painful. Governments – not always to their own advantage – have been hasty in replacing the white man by the national. The churches do not wish to seem behindhand in asserting their independence of the past, and their full participation in the process of Africanization.

These churches, however, are not the youngest in the world. The great churches in Papua–New Guinea, for instance, are of even more recent date. The majority of thoughtful Christians in that area seem prepared to accept for the time being the presence of the white man as necessary during the time of rapid development. The head of the Lutheran Church is already a born Papuan, and both the Roman Catholic and the Anglican fellowships have Papuan bishops.[2] All churches are aware of the need to hand over control as rapidly as this can be done. Already voices are heard suggesting that the process lags and should be accelerated. But there is general recognition that this will take time and should not be unduly hurried.

For all this, the subject is one of great importance in the Christian world, and deserves careful consideration.

To some extent, it must be admitted, missionaries themselves are to blame for a confrontation that could have been avoided if they had been more ready to read the signs of the times. Out of many possible causes of tension, four may be singled out:

[2] The Anglican Church in fact appointed its second Papuan bishop in December, 1975.

1. Missionaries have tended to be authoritarian in their attitudes. In the early days this was almost unavoidable. The missionary was the authority in the sense that he was the only man who knew, the only one who could read the Scriptures (in the days before the first translation into a local language had been made), and therefore the man who could give an answer to the innumerable questions asked by converts. The habit once learned is not easily unlearned.

2. Missionaries have not always been ready to encourage the desire of Christians, as education developed, to play a larger part in the leadership and direction of the life of the churches. Many promising young men and women who could have found a place in the life of the Church have found a career in government service, or in less formally ecclesiastical bodies such as the YMCA, feeling that there they would have a freedom likely to be denied them in the world of ecclesiastical bureaucracy.

3. Financial help from the west has all too often stood in the way of local independence. If decisions on important matters affecting the life and welfare of the Church have to be taken far away by a church board in the west, the members of which cannot possibly be aware of all the factors in the local situation, the price paid for the acceptance of that help may well seem too heavy in the eyes of those who want to get on with the job and make their own decisions.

4. In a number of cases the missionaries have undoubtedly stayed on too long; they have hesitated to trust the forces of the local church, and have believed themselves to be indispensable, when there were those ready to take their place and hold responsibilities for which the missionaries had considered them to be still unfitted. This has probably been the major factor in creating tensions which have hindered the growth and well-being of the churches. Sometimes, of course, the missionaries were right; there were also many cases in which they were wrong.

Whether we like it or not, then, there is the 'moratorium' claim. The questions raised by it are of more than temporary or merely local importance. The danger is that a settlement may be pressed for and accepted without consideration of the theological issues that arise; and these, if carefully considered, will be seen to go to the very roots of the nature of the Church and its calling in the world. From practical concerns we must now turn to the theological investigation.

2. The Nature of the Christian Task

What is the purpose for which God has brought into being the Church as the body of Christ?

A good starting-point for the consideration of this theme is provided by the documents of the Fourth World Missionary Conference held at Whitby, Ontario in 1947. This was the first meeting at which the full spiritual equality and independence of the third-world churches was taken as so axiomatic as not even to need discussion. At Edinburgh 1910, the third world had been present, but almost exclusively in the person of missionaries at work in that world. The expression 'younger churches' came into currency about the time of the Jerusalem Conference of 1928; at that time it was found to be acceptable, but later came to be abandoned as having about it an air of still-continuing western paternalism. At Tambaram 1938, by fiat of the great dictator John R. Mott, it was required that at least half of the representation of each area must be made up of members of indigenous churches, and that these were to come – in the expressive phrase of one of the Chinese delegates – as 'representatives and not as specimens'. At Whitby 1947, the 'younger churches' were there as of right, and on a footing of perfect equality.

This being so, the question put to the leaders of these churches by their friends from the west was the following: 'What are your plans for the total evangelization of your country?' It was at once clear that only the Koreans had been thinking in these terms. This was of course before the tragic events of the invasion and the total isolation from the rest of the world of Korea north of the 38th parallel.

The bearing of the question is clear. It does not mean, 'Is the church which you represent capable of maintaining itself in its present form without aid from the west?' In a number of cases this question had been tested out by the sad experiences of the war-time period, and a resoundingly affirmative answer had been given. But the bearing of the question posed at Whitby was very different. Are the churches in the third world, as they are now, able to consider the completion of the Christian task? How do the three per cent of the population in India which are Christian propose to bring the gospel to the ninety-seven per cent who are not? Or the one per cent in Japan to the ninety-nine? Or the tiny Church in Cambodia to evangelize the five million (now seven million) who have never heard the gospel?

An earlier generation might have answered the question in terms of evolutionary optimism. God has a million years to work out his purpose in the world; why all this hurry? We have perhaps learnt better with the passage of the years. The king's business does demand haste, though not precipitancy. Following Dr. Mott, we have come to realize that it is the business of each generation of Christians in this partially-Christianized world to make the gospel available (as far as that is possible) to the contemporary generation of non-Christians. When in 1961 the International Missionary Council was integrated with the World Council of Churches, the aim of the new Department of World Mission and Evangelism was stated to be 'to further the proclamation to the whole world of the gospel of Jesus Christ to the end that all men may believe and be saved'. A little later by the time of the conference held at Mexico City in 1963, there came about a general acceptance of the slogan: 'the whole Church bringing the whole gospel to the whole world.' This does not look to some dim eschatological future, but stresses once again the responsibility of each Christian generation for those contemporaries who are still outside the covenant made by God with men through Jesus Christ our Lord.

This means that, since Christ died for all, every man has the *right* to have the gospel so presented to him that he may be able to understand it and in the light of that understanding accept or reject it. This affirmation does not in any way deny the universal working of God in his world; it does stress the transcendent worth of Jesus Christ and condemns by implication the lethargy of those Christians who have failed to recognize the obligation to share this knowledge with all men, in east and west, in north and south.

There is a difference in the availability of the gospel in various parts of the world. In Britain we are faced with a decline in church attendance and an increasingly materialistic outlook among large sections of the population. It remains a fact that, if

50

it seemed good to the churches so to plan, it would be possible to arrange for every dwelling in the country to be visited within a month by convinced Christians concerned to share their knowledge with all who are ready to hear. The same is not true in Iran or in Thailand. Does this mean that there is a case for the international sharing of responsibility, and for a response by the whole Church to the challenge to make this gospel universally known, as far as the political circumstances of the time permit?

3. The Nature of the Church

The nature of the Church's task is a deduction from the nature of the Church itself. Inadequate practice can nearly always be traced back to an inadequate theology. If the churches have failed to respond to the challenge to make the gospel known, the reason may perhaps be found in an imperfect understanding of the nature of the Church itself as the body of Christ.

The best chapter of that uneven book *Honest to God*[3] was that which is called 'The Man for Others'. This is an excellent designation of Jesus Christ; he was, in fact, the man who never thought of himself or of his own interests, but poured himself out in service to others, until the last outpouring of life itself for the life of the world. If the Church is the body of Christ, it must also be the Church for others. William Temple well expressed this when he said that the Church is the only society in the world which exists for the benefit of those who are not members of it. This must not be pressed too far; the Church does of course serve also those who are members; but what makes it the Church of Jesus Christ is precisely that it does look beyond itself, and is always concerned for that which lies outside itself.

The Church has always found it difficult to bear in mind this aspect of its vocation.

It was all too easy for the churches in the west to become so absorbed in their own affairs – not to mention their own local controversies – as to forget that there was a world outside waiting for the gospel.

The same thing can happen so easily to a church which exists,

[3] Bishop John A. T. Robinson (SCM Press, 1963), chapter 4, pages 64–83.

perhaps on sufferance, in a mainly non-Christian world. This is what befell the very ancient Church of the Thomas Christians in South India. That group of Christians managed to survive for more than a thousand years in almost total isolation from the rest of the Christian world. This was a remarkable achievement. But a price had to be paid for it. Having secured a certain social position among the Hindus and a measure of economic prosperity, that Church withdrew entirely within the limits of its own dwelling and did nothing whatever to evangelize even its own neighbours, let alone undertake anything in the way of the evangelization of India as a whole. When the European peoples became aware of the existence of this ancient Church, they believed that it had been preserved in order that it might become the living centre from which the light of the gospel would spread out to the whole of India.[4] But it proved far more difficult than had been expected to bring back evangelistic zeal where it had so long been absent. To this day that ancient Church has responded only in very limited fashion to the challenge of non-Christian India. The evangelization of the sub-continent had to await the coming of the western forces and the release of evangelistic zeal from sources outside India itself.

Almost excessive stress has been laid in recent years on the principle that the instrument for evangelization is the Christian community itself, and that evangelistic work is partial and unbalanced if it becomes the concern of a few, neglected or disregarded by the majority. This is undoubtedly good theology; it can become effective only if the Christian community itself is aware, as that ancient Indian Church was not aware, of its responsibility and takes up the task which God has placed within its reach. If we were to await the kindling of zeal in Christian communities as a whole, there might have been no missionary work at all in the world today.

The true doctrine of a church in a mainly non-Christian country was set forth persuasively in the nineteenth century by two great missionary thinkers: Henry Venn, General Secretary of the Church Missionary Society in England, and the American Congregationalist Rufus Anderson. Almost at the same time these two men realized that the aim of a mission must be its own disappearance and its replacement by the church. They therefore

[4] See, for example, the *Christian Researches* of the Rev. Claudius Buchanan, based on his visit to Travancore in 1806.

set forth the idea of a church which would be self-governing, self-supporting and self-propagating. There were defects in their understanding of the situation; neither of the two men had ever been a missionary, and therefore they underestimated some of the problems in the way of the realization of their ideal. Yet they were on the right lines; a Christian body which remains dependent on outside help and which looks to some Christian body outside itself for support and nourishment can never grow out of the stage of infancy. A church is a church in the full sense of the term only when it can provide for all its own needs and reach out beyond itself in a concern for the needs of others.

Why did the ideal of these two thinkers fail to translate itself into practice in so many areas of the third world?

The reason may be sought in a defective theology on the part of a great many missionaries. Henry Venn complained that hardly any of those who worked under his benign guidance had any real idea of what a church is and should be. They failed to realize the true relationship between church and mission; they must have known that in some way out of the mission a church must grow; they seem hardly to have thought out what this would imply. Missionaries of the Church Missionary Society felt that their church was in England; instinctively they separated themselves from the Christians who had been gathered into the church under their care. American missionaries frequently retained membership in the church of their origin; they thus condemned themselves to be always strangers and visitors in the church in Asia or Africa which they served.

One of the first Christian thinkers to realize what a church must be in the third world was the great Bishop of Uganda, A. R. Tucker, towards the end of the nineteenth century. He saw that the missionary must regard himself as a servant of that church, must work within it and identify himself wholly with it, as long as his period of service might last. He found himself faced by solid opposition on the part of the missionaries who served under him. They felt that their primary loyalty was to the far-away church which had commissioned and sent them. How could a minister of the Church of England exchange that dignity for the position of minister of an African church, by which he had not been ordained and by which he was not supported? Dr. Louise Pirouet, who probably has a better knowledge of the records of that time than anyone else, has told me that the missionaries of that time realized that the formation of an African Church carried as its corollary the probability that in due course missionaries would find themselves serving under African leadership; this was a possibility which at the time they were not willing even to consider. (Less than fifty years later missionary candidates, including myself, were eager to serve in a 'native' Church, to be ordained within such a Church, and to give their unconditional service to it.)

The attitude of these missionaries indicates the extent to which mission and church had come to be regarded as separate entities. One result of this was that, when churches did begin to be formed in these newly developing countries, certain areas of the life of the church, particularly pastoral responsibilities, were handed over to the care and financial support of the church, while others, including most of the institutional work, and in many cases responsibility for evangelistic work, remained in the hands of the mission. This being so, the mission remained in control of the funds which came from the west, whereas the church was expected to subsist on the sometimes exiguous resources available from the local congregations. Inevitably the church came to be identified with the static in Christian service, and the mission with dynamic activity.

This was reinforced by the nature of the training given to those who were to be leaders in the Church. We shall consider later the problem of theological training in its relationship to leadership in the Church. In the early days, the missionaries transferred to their fields almost exactly the idea of the ministry with which they had been familiar in their own countries. For centuries in the west the ordained minister had been primarily the pastor, the shepherd of an identifiable and locally defined flock. The Anglican priest at his ordination is told that his task will be 'to teach and to premonish, to feed and provide for the Lord's family, to seek for Christ's sheep that are dispersed abroad, and for his children who are in the midst of this naughty world, that they may be saved through Christ for ever'. This noble ideal seems to imply evangelistic work outside the safe boundaries of the existing flock. But in practice the minister of an Anglican village congregation, though he might have to deal with refractory sheep of the flock, would have little occasion to cast his eyes beyond those boundaries and think of the 'other sheep' of whom Christ seems to speak in his high-priestly prayer (John

17). His concern as pastor was with those who in some sense at least were already within the flock.

Exactly the same ideal was transferred by the missionaries to those whom they were led to ordain or to present for ordination in their fields of service. These would be ordained as pastors, as soon as there was a flock for them to care for. For this they were trained, and this in most cases they regarded as their field of service. In the area committed to them there might be only 600 Christians as against 30,000 or more non-Christians; their field of operation (as they understood it) was to be the 'little flock'. There were, of course, exceptions. One old Indian friend told me that, in seven years of service in a largely non-Christian neighbourhood, he had preached in every village and in every street inhabited by non-Christians. But this was an exception. All too often the pastor, if asked whose was the responsibility for the 'other sheep', would reply: 'That is the responsibility of the mission; they have the funds and the personnel; we have a full-time job in looking after those who are already Christians.'

Once this fatal dichotomy of church and mission has been established, it is very difficult to correct it and to bring the church back to a true understanding of its nature. Self-interest, apathy, or timidity, can easily cause the church to withdraw inwards upon itself. The fostering of the inner life of the congregation is, obviously, one of the essential activities of the church. But this can go forward prosperously only if the other dimension, expansion into the world, is kept steadily before the eyes of the faithful. Experience shows that when a church grows by what Roland Allen called 'spontaneous expansion' – by the witness of one to one, by the testimony of the Christian family to its non-Christian relatives, by the service of unpaid evangelists, by the personal witness of those who have been set on fire by the love of Christ – the church is true to its own nature, manifests its being as the body of Christ, and so grows from strength to strength. Where this does not take place, introversion can only be another name for stagnation and decay.

It is important not to limit witness too narrowly to one type of Christian testimony. The gospel of Christ is to be proclaimed to all men everywhere. It is also to be proclaimed to men in every aspect of their being. There has always been a dangerous tendency to limit the relevance of the gospel to supposedly spiritual spheres, as though there could be any ultimate distinction between the sacred and the secular, the spiritual and the temporal. There was a time when it was claimed that the Church had nothing to say in the world of economics; all things in that realm, it was held, were governed by self-acting laws which could not be changed, and which in the end (through the natural harmony of interests) would work out to the common advantage, whatever might be the loss and suffering caused to individuals in the process of the working out of the laws. It was necessary for the Church to remind the economists that economic science does not in the last resort deal with supply and demand, prices and trade recessions, but with men and women at work; and that Christ is at all times concerned with people, whether at work or at play, in the factory or in the home. There are no autonomous realms, no areas of human life in which his writ does not run, no aspects of human life which are beyond the reach of his laws. For this insight we are permanently indebted to the Christian socialists. This has become so much a part of ordinary ecumenical thinking that there is no need to labour the point.

There is, however, a danger that the minds of Christians may become so occupied, indeed obsessed with economic and social problems that other dimensions of Christian witness may be obscured. The geographical factor is still there, and its existence will be overlooked at our peril. It is still a fact that one-third of the population of the world has never so much as heard the name of Jesus Christ, and that a further third, though it has heard the name, has never been confronted with the Christian message in a manner that would make possible a rational decision about its truth. The primary concern of the Church as mission must be with those who have never heard the Name. The twentieth century has made it much more difficult than the nineteenth for those who are outside the limits of the existing Church to hear the message. There are many whom the Church may not be able to reach by any method other than that of prayer. This fact does not alter the situation. The mission of the Church extends to the whole world of men to the ends of the earth and to the end of time. Any lowering of the sights of the Church is bound to have disastrous effects on its own life. If it ceases to be the Church for others, in the most comprehensive

56

sense of that term, then it is in danger of ceasing to be the Church of anyone at all.

So much for the nature of the Church. Within that broad perspective, we still have to ask in what sense exactly the mission of the Church as the proclaimer of the good news of God in Jesus Christ is to be understood and carried out under the conditions of our present time.

4. The Nature of Mission

We have already had occasion to note the harm done by inaccurate use of language; once again there is ground for complaint in the nondescript use of the term 'mission'.

In recent times the expression 'the mission of God' has been fairly widely used. But 'mission' is a passive form – it means *being sent*, and this is just what God can never be; he is always the sender; we can speak of the mission of the Son or of the Holy Spirit, but not of the mission of God.

Similarly some have referred to 'mission in six continents'. This expression seems to have been used at the meeting of the Department of Mission and World Evangelism held at Mexico City in 1963. The correct expression is of course 'witness in six continents', and this is in fact the title of the official report of that conference.[5] 'Mission in six continents' represents the desire of the third-world churches to deny any distinction between older and younger in the Christian world rather than any serious attempt at theological thought. If everything is mission, nothing is mission, and we are back in the night in which all cats are grey. The Johannine writings direct us to this great term 'witness', the comprehensive term to include every form of Christian activity, since every activity is directed to bearing witness to Christ as Lord, and can be so since he himself found the perfect expression of his activity in that he was the witness to the Father who had sent him. There is a unity in all Christian activity. At the same time there is great variety, since witness will take on very different forms according as it is directed to the sophisticated

[5] Edited by R. K. Orchard (London, 1964). Unfortunately the chapter by Bishop J. E. L. Newbigin in *The Ecumenical Advance*, ed. H. E. Fey (Westminster, 1970) – the second volume of the ecumenical history – does appear under the title 'Mission to Six Continents'.

society of the post-Christian world, to half-Christianized young people, or to those who have never heard a word of the gospel of Jesus Christ.

If we turn to the New Testament, we shall find that activities of the Christian Church fall under the three headings of worship, edification and extension. *Worship* is the life of the Church directed upwards to God who is the source of all good things. Edification (*oikodome*), upbuilding, represents the life of the Church directed inwards, in instruction, fellowship, mutual service, and the elimination of all evil things which mar the unity and purity of the life of the fellowship. *Extension* is the Church going forth from itself, becoming in truth the Church for others as it moves out of the safety of its own inner organization into the world outside, seeking nothing for itself, but desiring only that others should come to the knowledge of that truth by which the Church lives.

We should take note, within this work of extension, of one distinction which is recognized in the New Testament. There is first the mission to Israel; then there is the mission to the Gentiles (*ta ethne*). We find this distinction clearly set out in Galatians 2:8–10: 'He who worked through Peter for the mission to the circumcision [Israel] worked through me also for the Gentiles . . . that we should go to the Gentiles, and they to the circumcised.' Israel is related to God in the covenants given through Abraham and through Moses. All men, Gentiles included, are within the universal covenant made with the human race in Noah (Gen. 9:8–17).[6] Christians are heirs of both these covenants; but they alone have the special vocation involved in the new covenant relationship between God and man established by Jesus Christ through his blood. Into this new relationship all men are to be brought through the proclamation of the gospel and the response of faith.

Both these missions are of permanent obligation.

The mission to Israel has to be carried out with the utmost prudence and delicacy. Since the Holocaust, as the Jews call the appalling events which took place in Germany under Hitler, in which something like six million Jews perished, it has been

[6] Note especially 9:9 – 'I now make my covenant with you and with your descendants after you'; and 9:12 – 'the covenant which I establish between myself and you and every living creature with you, to endless generations'. (New English Bible.)

doubly difficult for Christians to speak a word to Jews in the name of Christ. Even the name 'Christ' is better avoided; to the Christian it speaks of our reconciliation to God through him who is the Messiah, to the Jew it conveys the memory of centuries of oppression and persecution. We can speak to our Jewish friends of Jesus of Nazareth whom they can recognize as a fellow Jew. Yet even the suggestion that any Jew needs to be converted to the Jesus whom Christians profess arouses the most violent feelings of resentment. For all that, the attitude of the Jew towards this same Jesus in the twentieth century is astonishingly different from that of his ancestors even in the nineteenth century. Then, as we are told in a pamphlet by Rabbi S. Sandmel,[7] Jews 'have either not wanted to know about him in any way, or else have thought that some knowledge about him, if even slightly favourable, might seem to amount to disloyalty to Judaism'. Contrast with this view the remarkably fair and temperate article on him in the recently published *Encyclopaedia Judaica*. The Jews have rediscovered Jesus as the greatest of all Jews. They are determined to understand and to present him in their way, not as he has been pictured by Christians and as he has been misunderstood by Jews in the past.[8] The Christian can but pray that, through this new contact with an unknown man, they may be led to find that the Messiah for whom they look is the Messiah who has already come.

The mission to *ta ethne* does not imply any claim to western superiority. After all, it is not so long ago that our own people were themselves *ethne*, practising human sacrifice and other not very edifying rites. This mission does not deny the working of God among all those nations whom he has held in the hollow of his hand and whom he has kept within his covenants of creation and providence. It simply takes the New Testament seriously, basing itself on the affirmation that Christ died for all in order that all men may die to themselves to live in him in the light of the new covenant that he has made with them in his death and resurrection. That mission will remain an obligation resting on the Church until time as we now know it comes to an end and the new age begins. It is mission 'to the ends of the earth and to the end of time'.

[7] S. Sandmel, *A Jewish View of Jesus* (London, 1975).
[8] As an interesting example of this tendency we may note the work of G. Vermes, *Jesus the Jew* (Collins, 1973).

If mission is understood in this sense, many absurdities and confusions can be avoided.

More than a century ago the Church Missionary Society in India began to give 'missionary status' to educated converts. Thus 'missionary' was turned from function into status. The Indian missionary would sit on the 'mission council' from which so far all 'natives' had been excluded. A fatal barrier was erected between him and his humbler brethren who were merely 'pastors' with no share in the privileges accorded to the elect.

In 1922 an enthusiastic British delegate to the meeting of the World Student Christian Federation held in Peking came back announcing to the world that China would before long be sending missionaries to Britain. The intention was excellent; the phrasing was absurd. Chinese Christians have profoundly impressed the west by their ability and devotion. At the Tambaram Conference of 1938 it was agreed by all that the most outstanding delegation was that from China. But the use of the word 'missionary' in this connexion was just another illustration of the facile misuse of words without any clear understanding of their meaning.

It would greatly help to avoid confusion if we could agree to distinguish between three different types of Christian outreach, each of which is part of the one great operation, but differs in many ways from the other two.

The first should be called Church extension. This is the term to use for work where a firm Christian base has been established, and the gospel is readily available in spoken and printed word to any who may desire to hear it. This is the situation over the greater part of the western world, even in so deeply dechristianized a city as Hamburg. There are many places in the third world also where this level of availability has been reached. For instance, in Nairobi, a city of slightly more than half a million people, half the population is Christian at least in name. Churches abound. The whole Bible is available in all the main languages of the area. Christian witness in such a city does not necessarily involve any crossing of a cultural or linguistic frontier. All that is needed for the spread of the Christian gospel is that ministers of Christian churches and members of their congregations should care enough about their faith to wish to share it with their neighbours. The problem is not that of accessibility of the gospel, but of creating in the minds of those who are not at present interested a desire for the knowledge of God in Christ, and of finding the idiom in which the gospel can be made intelligible to modern man and relevant to his needs.

In such a situation, the ordinary minister of the gospel is the indigenous Christian. Help from a foreigner is not excluded, indeed may be desirable, if there is a serious disparity in educational level between the Christian witnesses and those whom they are seeking to reach. But this must be regarded as the exception rather than the rule.

The second main area of extension should properly be called inter-church aid. Here the implication is that a church has already been well established, but still asks that its resources may be strengthened by help from outside. One obvious field is that of theological education. Even in so advanced an area as South India, where the number of competent Indian theologians is steadily increasing, the theological institutions are glad to have the help of colleagues from the west, for longer or for shorter periods. In this field two-way traffic is possible, and indeed is well established. Union Theological Seminary in New York has long had a professorship specially intended to make it possible for scholars from the third world to spend a year as fully accredited professors of that distinguished institution. Many other institutions have proved the value of having for a year or more a colleague from overseas.

What is to be noted about such service (in whichever direction it takes place) is that it is rendered within the context of the Church and that it is directed primarily to those who are already Christians. A teacher in a theological school lives in a Christian community. From week's end to week's end he may not see a single non-Christian, although if he is wise he will move out as often as possible from the Christian into the non-Christian environment. Ordinarily the theological teacher will be carrying out his work in his own language, so there will be no linguistic barrier to cross. Indeed the work expected of him will not be markedly different from that which he might be doing in his own country, except that he must be aware all the time of the need to understand the mind of students whose background is very different from his own and to adapt his teaching, as far as he is able, to their needs.

If this terminology could be accepted, it would be possible to restore to the terms 'mission' and 'missionary' their correct and biblical meaning. What makes these specific is not the crossing of a geographical or cultural frontier, but the crossing of a covenant line. The Christian missionary is one who goes to those who have never been brought within the new covenant relationship between God and man established by Jesus Christ.

For a Christian it is a terrible experience to find himself the only Christian in a city of perhaps fifty thousand people. Deeply convinced as he may be of the sovereignty of Jesus Christ over all men and of his concern for those who have never heard of him, he is yet aware of the way in which that sovereignty is denied in everything that he sees and hears around him. In such a situation he finds nothing exaggerated in the words of Paul, 'I could wish that I myself were accursed and cut off from Christ for the sake of my brethren'. (Rom. 9:3, RSV). There is literally nothing that he would not do to bring Christ to those who do not know him.

It is not for us to attempt to determine the status in the sight of God of those who are related to him only through the universal covenant. But it is simply fact that there is a great difference between one who has never heard the Name of Jesus Christ and one who has heard that Name and accepted it as the Name of the Saviour. To reach such people does often involve a journey and the crossing of linguistic and cultural frontiers. But these are not the essential constituents in the missionary task. Nor should it be supposed that the missionary need always be a white man. Among those who have brought the gospel to the peoples of Africa the name of Canon Apolo Kivebulaya will always stand high. Few would deny to him the title 'missionary'. In point of fact, in order to become a missionary he had only to make quite a short journey. But when he made contact with the pygmy peoples in the eternal rain forest of what is now Zaïre, they were to him an entirely unknown people, and he was almost as much a foreigner to them as a white man would have been. What made him a missionary was his deep concern to share with others what he had known of Christ, and especially to make him known in places where his name had never previously been uttered. Like Paul he did not wish to build upon another's foundation.

We have noted already the stress laid in many circles on the Christian community as the instrument of evangelization. Well and good where a Christian community exists. A new problem arises where there is no Christian community and the Christian stands alone. It may well happen that the Christian has to make his own the utterance of the Church Father Tertullian that there are situations in which the single Christian *is* the Holy Catholic Church. The tiny group of missionaries may have to be and to create the fellowship of the Church, and to believe that gradually others will be drawn in until there is at least the nucleus of a fellowship growing out of the soil and not an exotic introduced from an alien world. Of course the group is supported by the prayers of those who have sent them out. Unless they are particularly bad at making friends, they will soon have friends among those whom they hope to win for Christ. And they may experience in a peculiarly intimate way the companionship of the risen Christ.

It is to be observed that this is a situation which still obtains over a considerable part of the earth's surface. This is what we are really talking about when we discuss missions. What an earlier generation called by a rather unhappy military metaphor 'the unoccupied fields' are the first priority in all matters of missionary strategy. In relation to them the Lord is still saying, 'Whom shall we send and who will go for us?' We will postpone till the last chapter the question who should go and by whom they should be sent. For the moment our only concern is to establish an order of priorities and to attempt to reach some lucidity in a discussion that has often become gravely confused. To distinguish between these three types of Christian service is not to say that one is more valuable. Each has its place; in the present situation of the churches it can be maintained without much fear of contradiction that each will gain in efficiency and strength if it is an expression of the international character of the Church, and of fellowship in the service of Christ of those who come from different backgrounds and represent a variety of experiences within the Christian fellowship.

5. Identity with What?

It remains to consider the meaning, in a Christian connexion, of the word 'identity' which has become part of the contemporary jargon. We are told that a church in the third world cannot discover, or recover its identity as long as the situation is confused by the presence of foreigners. Let the foreigner withdraw, perhaps for a time, perhaps for ever; the situation will then be eased and the question of identity can be more calmly and dispassionately faced.

No one is likely to deny that rootlessness is one of the major problems with which the world is faced today. As in the period of the early industrial revolution in Europe, millions of people all over the world are pouring into the cities in the often disappointed expectation of a better and fuller life. They find themselves released from many of the old disciplines of tribal life and from the complex structure that in a thousand ways supported them in their previous existence. They have to face endless problems of adjustment to new conditions, which in many cases they are ill equipped to make. Foreign rule, education in a foreign language, the infliction of foreign cultures, the foreign mass media, the availability of foreign goods to the use of which they had not previously been accustomed – all these things make deep inroads into the minds and hearts of people who had hardly been prepared at all for these revolutionary changes. Not unnaturally the victim is inclined to say with the poet: 'I a stranger and afraid In a world I never made.' To have no home and to feel that one has no home is a devastating experience. The old identity has been lost; where is a new identity to be found? Only in rare cases can the wanderer return to the life which he had abandoned and adapt himself without friction to its requirements; the mine-worker who comes back to his old home in Lesotho or Mozambique is not the man who set out a year or eighteen months before.

As in other sections, the first task here is to attempt to ascertain exactly what it is that we are talking about.

The fact is that all of us have a variety of identities, and that these are divisive in relationship to others who do not share the same group identity, though promoting the cohesion of those who are within that particular group.

In contemporary thinking, colour plays an unduly large part in providing stereotypes. We constantly hear the expression 'the white man', as though this provided any clear clue as to an identity. Every white man has other identities which bear no relation to colour. Even 'European' is an identity which we have difficulty in working out. Is Great Britain a part of Europe or not? The answer to this question was so doubtful that the socialist government in Britain was prepared to flout every principle of constitutional propriety and hold a referendum to decide the issue. The British people reasserted their common sense and decided that it is. Britain is some kind of a geographical unity, and the greater part of the British Isles are included in the United Kingdom of Great Britain and Northern Ireland. But at the moment there are loud cries demanding that the separate identity of Scotland and Wales be recognized. Some members of the population regard themselves as belonging to the 'working class'; others submit to being included in that non-existent entity, the 'middle class'. We have religious and other identities. I live in Oxford, but that does not make me an Oxford man. And so on and so on endlessly. The plain fact is that our individual identity has an existence only at the meeting point of many other identities.

There is much talk today of the African identity, the African personality, and so on. This is natural, but is misleading if taken as anything other than a reference to a geographical land mass. Ethiopia has little in common with Zambia, English-speaking Nigeria with French-speaking Chad. There is no unity of African culture, even to the extent that Europe can be said to share a common culture. In a number of Bantu groups, circumcision of both boys and girls plays a very important part. The neighbouring Nilotic peoples reject circumcision as a meaningless and unnecessary mutilation. The danger is that the idea of an African identity could be created on a purely negative basis: dislike of the white man and all his ways. The way from the negative to the positive is often hard to find.

A backward-looking search for identity may conceal other dangers. The past of the African or Asian may have been based on a tribal identity. If so, the recovery of this partial but intensely experienced identity might hinder the development of that more broadly-based identity into which we seem to be called in our shrinking world. Africa was parcelled out by the colonial powers into multi-tribal colonies; these absurd frontiers have persisted with very little change into the epoch of the newly-created independent states. Unity has been achieved; but not far below the surface old tribal feelings and sometimes jealousies persist. In Rhodesia the Matabele and the Mashona have never loved one another. They may for the moment be united in opposition to the white ruler; will they later be able to coalesce in the creation of a genuinely united and independent African state? Some years ago I remarked to a Nigerian, 'I think that you are a Yoruba'. He replied, 'As a matter of fact I am; but we don't think much these days about that kind of thing. We prefer to be regarded as all Nigerians together'. This was not long before the outbreak of the disastrous civil war. The massacres of Ibo people in Northern Nigeria had led to a tremendous resurgence of tribal feeling, to the demand for an independent Biafra, and so to a long-continued and destructive war. It is good that a generous and high-minded government is setting itself to heal the wounds that occurred during the gloomy years of hostility.

The Church has not been successful in keeping itself free from tribal and local loyalties. One diocese in the Church of South India is preparing to divide into two; the cause for this is caste-loyalty rather than any reason based on Christian conviction or theology. In Kenya the Anglican Church was saved from a tribal identity by the accident that missionaries came in from both Uganda and up from the coast; the Church sprawls right across the country. And yet even here the intense tribal self-consciousness of the Kikuyu has led to the suggestion of a separate Kikuyu-speaking province in which the existing unity of the Church would be lost.

The Presbyterian Church of East Africa is by contrast predominantly the Church of a single people. It was a blow to the ecumenical cause when that Church withdrew from the committee which was discussing the possibility of Church union in East Africa. The intimate sense of identity within a single church and people was at war with the plan for a wider identity of church and people. It is good, however, that we can record the subsequent withdrawal of this mistaken decision.

Illustrations could be drawn from every part of the world, including Europe. No people other than the English could have produced anything so odd as the Church of England. I have heard that notable Scotsman Dr. Carnegie Simpson express in public his amazement that among a people so intelligent as the English Presbyterianism had made so little headway. My astonishment is that among a people so intelligent as the Scots the Episcopal Church is still so small. And so we could go on with our tribal banter and disputes.

There is, however, a very serious side to this whole question.

As Christians we are called to assert the great principle that our essential identity is to be found in Jesus Christ and nowhere else. This was the experience of the Church in its earliest days. Some were seeking to maintain a Jewish identity, and others to maintain the independence of a Gentile identity. Between them they nearly succeeded in destroying the Church. This was what the great confrontation between Peter and Paul at Antioch was all about. Paul has expressed for us the result of that confrontation in moving words: 'as many of you as were baptized into Christ have put on Christ. There is neither Jew nor Greek, there is neither slave nor free, there is neither male nor female; for you are all one in Christ Jesus' (Gal. 3:27-28, RSV). This becomes an essential part of the teaching on the Church given in the Epistle to the Ephesians: 'he is our peace, who has made us both one, and has broken down the dividing wall of hostility ... that he might create in himself one new man in place of the two, so making peace' (Eph. 2:14-15, RSV). When the new identity in Christ has been established, there can be no further question of division or of hostility.

This has been the experience of the Church in all ages. In proportion as we are rooted in Christ, we can reach out to find our brother. The sense of foreignness disappears and is replaced by a profound experience of our oneness in Christ. When this is given all other differences are insignificant in comparison; they are no longer divisive, but interesting and enriching. It is unlikely that Christians will ever think exactly the same things on all subjects or behave in exactly the same way. It would be very tedious if they did. There is charm in variety, and the variety of Christian insights is certainly part of the riches of the Church. Even deep disagreements on questions of politics or social order, or (within limits) on questions of theological interpretation, need not mar the harmony. Humility demands that we be willing to learn from those with whom we disagree. Only when hatred and arrogance make their way back into the Christian fellowship is the unity broken.

'Our church will never accept the idea of a purely African Church. This would go directly contrary to the ideal of the catholic church into which we have been trying to help our province to grow.' So one of the Anglican bishops in Kenya wrote recently. This is good theology. When the basic unity, the new identity in Christ is guaranteed, the presence of the foreigner is felt neither as hindrance nor as embarrassment. The presence of black and white and brown in a single church is a perpetual reminder of the truth that Christ has really died for all, and that in so far as any man or group really lives at all, that man or that group lives in the unity of the new humanity which has come into being through the death and resurrection of Jesus Christ.

4

REVOLUTIONARY ACTIVITY FOR ALL?

As long as the WCC and the churches which are its members maintain the conviction that faith demands obedience, that obedience adds not a jot to faith but is the necessary consequence of faith, then there will not be two ecumenisms, the one vertical and the other horizontal, meeting from time to time and exchanging courtesies; there will be only one ecumenism, at once spiritual and temporal, at once anxious for true faith and eager for bold action, living in expectation of the new heaven and new earth and, because of this very expectation, vitally concerned to make this earth livable for all humankind.

In these words, taken from a review of the World Council's Handbook *Uppsala to Nairobi* (SPCK, 1975), Professor Roger Mehl of the University of Strasbourg sums up with characteristic French clarity the major issue which has concerned and troubled all friends of the World Council over the last ten years or so. A vertical ecumenism which does not find its outlet in active obedience becomes introverted and pietistic. A horizontal ecumenism which does not look upwards to its source becomes merely humanitarian without inspiration and without divine illumination. Has the World Council managed to keep the two in such equilibrium that there is in fact only one ecumenism, or have the paths so widely diverged that the original unity of Faith and Order with Life and Work has now been finally dissolved?

It is at the point of political conviction and activity that this question has reached burning-point; this was naturally central both in the preparations for the Nairobi Assembly and in the discussions which took place during and after the sessions of that Assembly.

1. The Church and Politics

'Let the Church keep out of politics.' 'Keep politics out of the Church.' Is either of these solutions to the problem practicable? If practicable, would it be desirable?

69

On one interpretation of the words, the response in each case would be affirmative. There is hardly any situation in which it would be good that the Church should identify itself with one political party to the exclusion of all others. On the continent of Europe it had become traditional in almost every country that the Roman Catholic Church should organize its own political party, notable among them the centre party in Prussia. This practice seems almost everywhere to have been abandoned. There was a time in which it could be said that the Church of England was simply the conservative party at prayer. It is to the good of the common polity that so close an identification of one church with one party has become only a historical memory. The contrary claim that every Christian must necessarily be a socialist would not meet with general approbation.

So far we may agree that a separation between the Church and political commitment is desirable. This does not alter the fact that in many countries, though not in all, Christians do have political responsibilities, and that whether we like it or not politics do have a way of intruding themselves into the affairs of the churches. Liberty of religious worship and practice is enshrined in the universal declaration of human rights; but not all nations have subscribed that declaration, and not all of those who have signed it are as scrupulous as they should be in the observance of the principles laid down in it. Politics and religion cannot be kept as completely separate as some theorists would wish.

What then should be the attitude of Christians towards politics?

In the first half of the nineteenth century it was taken for granted in Britain that political activity was a necessary expression of Christian obedience. The evangelical reformers of that period were men of influence and in many cases members of Parliament. The House of Commons seemed to them to be the place above all others in which a Christian witness had to be borne and the Christian battle fought out. But towards the end of the century, both in Britain and in the United States, a polarization began to take place, as a result of which the Christian tended to withdraw into specifically religious areas, and the process of political and social reform fell into the hands of those who had no particular religious interest. This polarization was operative also within the Church, as those who called themselves liberals and those who called themselves conservatives found they were embarked on diverging, and sometimes conflicting understandings of the Christian gospel.

The story of events in the United States is both interesting and illuminating. The most original contribution of the United States to theological thinking so far has been the movement commonly called the Social Gospel. The pioneer of this movement, Walter Rauschenbusch, was very far from being either a revolutionary in politics or an extreme liberal in theology; his prayers, for example, show an excellent balance between a profound apprehension of the meaning of the Christian gospel and an equally profound concern for social righteousness, in a society in which the rights of the poor seemed to be almost wholly disregarded.[1] As the movement progressed 'evangelical' Christians (always inclined to conservatism in politics) came to feel that the programme of the movement for social and political change was being substituted for the message of personal salvation. Their natural reaction was to affirm that the sole business of the Church was to save souls; social and political change can be safely left where they rightly belong – in the hands of the politicians. In any case the only way to change social conditions is to change people – all social problems have their roots in the hearts and lives of unconverted people; until these are dealt with, no social change has any chance of permanent effects on society. By reaction against this attitude, many liberals were driven into detachment from the Church, feeling it to be an instrument of social stagnation and opposition to necessary change.

Both these attitudes persist in the Christian world today and account in part for that polarization of 'ecumenical' and 'evangelical' which is one of the major concerns in any study of the contemporary church situation.

Many voices are raised today to tell us that, as Christians, we should take an active part in the politics of the country of which we happen to be citizens, and also that we should try to obtain such a share of the spirit of prophecy as will enable us to detect the activity of God not only in the affairs of the churches, but also in the great historical movements of our times. This demand is not unreasonable. Christianity is a historical religion,

[1] See especially his books *Christianity and the Social Crisis* (1907) and *A Theology for the Social Gospel* (Abingdon Press, 1917).

both in the sense that it has a historical founder, Jesus Christ, and also in that history is seen as the sphere in which God is at work for the redemption of his world. To understand exactly how God is at work at any particular time is not easy; but perhaps it is a task that should be attempted. The prophets of Israel did interpret the history of their own times in the light of God's providence. We are reminded that Isaiah saw God at work in the rise of Assyria to imperial power, and could use that power for his own purposes: 'Ah, Assyria, the rod of my anger, the staff of my fury! Against a godless nation I send him'.[2] Similarly the general policy of the monotheist Cyrus to send exiles back to their own countries is interpreted by the prophet as a special grace given by the God of Israel to his now penitent people.

When contemporary Christians attempt to exercise this gift of prophetic interpretation, their attempts tend to show all too clearly how much we are limited by time and circumstance, and how hard it is really to ascend the mount of prophecy. At a consultation recently held in the United States and recorded in the *Christian Century* for November 24, 1974, one working party felt itself able to declare roundly that 'the liberation movement led by Mao Tse-tung falls within what Christians understand as God's saving work in history'. Other groups were not prepared to go so far, recognizing more clearly than others the enormous injustices by which the liberation movement has been accompanied. But the general summing-up was as follows: 'The achievements of the Chinese revolution somehow reflect what Christians mean by God's action in history. China's secular revolution is seen to have dimensions which some would call "saving acts of God"'. There is much virtue in that 'somehow' and that 'some'. In Scripture, salvation and righteousness are always closely associated. No secular revolution can be interpreted in these terms. It is the righteousness of God which must be vindicated by the deliverance of his people; the purpose of that deliverance is that the redeemed people may serve God

[2] Isaiah 10:5. Unfortunately those who quote the prophecy rarely read it through to the end. It goes on (verses 7, 16): 'But he does not so intend . . . Therefore the Lord, the Lord of hosts, will send wasting sickness among his stout warriors, and under his glory a burning will be kindled, like the burning of fire.' (RSV.)

according to the ordinances: 'How can we sing the Lord's song in a strange land?' (Psalm 137:4). The kingdom of God is not the same as any kingdom of man.

These contemporary utterances make it easy for us to understand how it was possible a century ago for Christians of equal intelligence and sincerity to interpret the advance of the colonial powers in Asia and elsewhere as among the saving acts of God. The observer in India could see signs of God's action on every hand. The country had been unified and universal peace established. Customs such as *sati* (the burning of Hindu widows on their husbands' pyres) and *thuggee* (the ritual murder of innocent travellers) had been brought to an end. Education and medical aid were being provided on a scale previously deemed impossible. The position of women had notably improved – for the first time an Indian woman had graduated from an Indian University. A beginning had been made with the emancipation of the depressed classes through education and the opening to them of careers from which they had earlier been excluded by social barriers. The Famine Code, one of the noblest policies ever set on foot by a civilized government, had laid down elaborate precautions to free the country from a scourge which had afflicted it from the earliest times. Where, if not in the law of God, was the inspiration that lay behind all these things to be found? It is unlikely that anyone today would take quite so favourable a view of the situation. The general opinion seems to be that the subjection of one people to another is in itself so grave a wrong as to outweigh any subsidiary benefits that may arise from such a subjection. Christians generally take this view of the six centuries of Islamic colonial control in Spain and Portugal, a period much longer than that which the Indian historian K. M. Panicker has taught us to call the Vasco da Gama era. During that period Spain and Portugal probably enjoyed a higher civilization than the rest of Europe; yet the Christian world heaved a sigh of relief when the colonial period finally came to an end with the liberation of these countries from Muslim rule.

We are all men of our own day and generation, and judge of things as we see them without the benefit of hindsight. It is likely that a century from now critics will look back with astonishment on the naïvety of those who, looking only at the outward benefits conferred by the rule of Mao Tse-tung, entirely overlooked

73

the diminution of the human substance which has so far shown itself everywhere as the inevitable accompaniment of a Marxist régime. It was Martin Niemöller, a man not unduly predisposed against Marxism, who said some years ago after a visit to Russia, 'The problem in Russia is simply that of remaining human'. These things may become more evident as the years pass.

2. Politics and the Third-World Churches

The work of the Christian missionary has entailed special problems of involvement and detachment.

The current mythology is that the Christian cause came in with the colonial powers and would depart with them, and that the missionary was so deeply involved in the policies of western powers as to have become, perhaps without knowing it, an instrument of oppression. Years of patient research will have to pass before the mythology is finally replaced by history. For the moment three cautionary remarks may be inserted:

1. In a great many countries the missionaries were there long before the colonial powers. They went out far beyond the limits of consular protection; if they were killed, as sometimes happened, the nation to which they belonged took no retaliatory action, and made no demand for compensation for their death.[3]

2. The majority of missionaries worked in countries other than those over which their own country exercised colonial control. In 1900 there were more American missionaries in India than British; to these have to be added Dutch, German, Swiss, Belgian, Swedish and representatives of many other nations. These were debarred from political activity, but were able to exercise a highly independent judgement on the policies and actions of the colonizing powers.

3. In many cases the missionaries resisted colonial occupation as long as this was possible. When they yielded, it was usually because the local authorities were no longer able to control the situation, and it seemed best to let moderately good white

[3] A partial exception to this generalization was France, which did in a number of cases demand reparation and especially in China imposed harsh and wounding terms.

men come in to save the weaker nations from extermination at the hands of wicked white men or equally wicked Arab slave-traders.

When the white man did come in with military and political authority, the missionaries were faced with a painful dilemma. Three possible courses lay open to them:

1. They could disclaim responsibility, quit the field and leave those whom they had come to love and serve helpless in the face of the new situation. When the French occupied Tahiti, the English missionaries found it wiser to leave the country. (But they did arrange as soon as possible for the work to be taken over by the Paris Evangelical Mission, an arrangement which has lasted to the present day with excellent effects.) In more recent times the White Fathers decided to withdraw all their missionaries from Mozambique, feeling themselves to be fatally compromised by the relationship between the Roman Catholic Church and a government of which they could not approve. Since then the situation in Mozambique has radically changed; it is possible that the Fathers feel today that their action was precipitate.

2. They could encourage their people to engage in what was bound to be futile resistance to the occupying power.

3. They could remain and do their best to act as intermediaries between the new rulers and the people, explaining to the former the ideas and the customs of a people of whom they knew nothing, and to the latter the intentions of the newcomers who according to international law were bound to rule in the interests of their subjects. This the missionaries were particularly well qualified to do, since they possessed a knowledge of the local language to which few other westerners could lay claim, and to some extent at least could live simultaneously in the two worlds involved.

Opinions will differ as to whether missionaries were wise to accept the third of these alternatives. There was always the danger that they might become so much involved in matters of state or government as to lose sight of the primary objective of their work. As governments became increasingly interested in education and other forms of social service, and found it convenient to get the missions to do most of the work for them, a missionary might find himself almost in the position of a civil servant, without the independence necessary for an impartial mediator. Cases are known to me from West Africa in which the entire salary of a missionary was paid by government for doing work of which the government approved – a situation which could not be other than spiritually perilous. When governments began to appoint missionaries to legislative councils and other similar official bodies, to represent 'native' interests, no doubt they acted sincerely. Not unnaturally the 'natives' came to wonder whose interests the missionaries were really there to serve.

Now all that has gone. The heyday of colonialism lasted in India for almost exactly a century, – over the greater part of Africa for very much less than that. On the whole the missionaries have welcomed the changed situation. They felt themselves relieved of the heavy burden of being supposed to possess a vast influence with the ruling power, which in reality had no existence at all. They were weary of being accused by nationally-minded friends of imperialist leanings of which they knew themselves to be entirely innocent. Some may have felt that the journey to political independence had been made too rapidly, and that a longer period of co-operation would have been beneficial to all concerned. But every one of them has accepted the new situation as it has come about. Some have decided to abandon their old citizenship and to accept citizenship in the country which they have made their home. Others have preferred to remain as guests and foreigners. But all have remained. They have adapted themselves with surprising ease to the changes in state and Church which have so rapidly come about, and have carried on with their work, whatever it might happen to be. Not one, whether Roman Catholic or Protestant, has left a position of trust and responsibility solely by reason of the political changes which have accompanied the disappearance of the colonial epoch.[4]

[4] Some missionaries felt that they would serve their people better by withdrawing than by staying. The continued presence of some others was made impossible by the new governments. But in the course of twenty-five years of rather close observation of the situation, I have not come across a single case of the missionary who decided just to get up and go.

Now responsibility for Christian witness in the social, political and international spheres has passed from the foreigner to the national. How far have the churches of the third world responded to the challenge of the new situation?

In India, in the early days of independence, there was considerable participation by Christians in political affairs at a high level. The first minister of health for the whole of independent India was the Christian lady, the Rajkumari Ameit Kaur. Her brother Rajah Sir Maharaj Singh was the first governor of Bombay after independence. A stalwart Baptist Dr. Mukerjee became governor of West Bengal. Japan has had Christian prime ministers. The first chief minister of Papua–New Guinea is a universally respected Roman Catholic. Yet there are signs that Christian involvement in public life is less than it was in the first years after independence came, perhaps because of a hardening of anti-Christian feeling in some newly independent countries, perhaps through a change in Christian attitudes towards service in a world in which it can never be easy to maintain Christian standards of integrity.

Many of the third-world churches have had their origins in pietistic missions, which have maintained the ideal of separation from the world rather than involvement in it. The task of the Christian, so it is believed, is to 'keep himself unspotted from the world' (James 1:27). How can he do so, if he makes the pursuit of a career in the world his major objective? The call to the Christian to come out and be separate rings out quite clearly in the New Testament (2 Cor. 6:17). What has a Christian to do with any of these worldly things?

It is perhaps this attitude which accounts for the fact that, though the great majority of African political leaders have received their training in mission schools and have been baptized, few today are practising Christians. Only one (as far as I know) has rejected his Christian faith in favour of Islam, but many are indifferent and regard it as more important to be abreast of the tide of Africanism, *négritude*, than to follow up the possibility that the gospel has something to say to the African situation today.

If asked why they have ceased to be Christians in anything but name, a number of these leaders answer frankly, 'The Church is not interested in the things that interest us – the acquisition of independence which is more than a sham, resistance to a

77

neo-colonialism which may be even more harmful than the political domination of the past; the building up of a national spirit; the recovery of identity' and so on. Such leaders, like Milton, 'cannot praise a fugitive and cloistered virtue'. They do not accept the rigid separation between the sacred and the profane, the spiritual and the worldly, which seems to characterize Christianity as they have known it and to run directly contrary to that primal vision of the African world, in which a distinction between the sacred and the secular is unknown.

3. To Make Oppression Bitter

Sadly we have to recognize that there is no such thing as a just society; there seems to be an inbuilt tendency in human affairs for justice to slide over into injustice. Even in free democratic societies, such as those of Britain and the Scandinavian countries, Christians have to be ceaselessly on the watch lest the interests of those who cannot speak for themselves – the old, the sick, handicapped children and the rest – be overridden by the self-interest of the strong, and lest the callousness of councils and committees work irrevocable havoc on the beauty of God's world.

If this is true in free societies, much more is it the case in those areas where the policy of government seems to be set in the direction of the limitation or suppression of human freedom. It is not difficult to make a long list of such areas.

We have given credit to the government of independent India for the law which has abolished untouchability. But legal enactment cannot always change situations, and the new legal freedom granted to the eighty million members of the scheduled communities does not seem to have become everywhere a reality; every day the Indian press records outrages committed against these people by those of higher caste, especially where the suppressed groups have been trying to insist upon their rights. In Malaysia the declared policy of Malaysianization seems to the Chinese in that country to threaten them with the loss of their language, and the extreme pressure on many to become Muslims appears to endanger the principle of religious liberty. The abominable treatment accorded to Asians in East Africa accords ill with declarations of democratic liberty.

President Amin has proclaimed his sympathy with the oppressed inhabitants of Scotland and Wales and has promised them his help in their struggle for freedom. The tiny island of Anguilla has declared in favour of independence from its larger neighbour St. Lucia. Even peaceful Switzerland has its independence movement; the French-speaking inhabitants of the Bernese Jura want liberation from the German-speaking 'gentlemen in Berne'. I have not heard whether the World Council of Churches has come out strongly in favour of this oppressed minority!

Three areas especially have drawn the attention of the world in general – the Blacks in the United States, South Africa and Latin America.

The campaign in favour of civil rights has markedly changed the situation in the United States. But for many Blacks in that country all that has been achieved is only a beginning and not an end. Black Power remains a symbol and an ideal, though visions of what is yet to be achieved may remain somewhat cloudy.

In South Africa there is one central point in the problems of race and colour. A government representing only a minority of the white electorate is convinced that it has the right and the Christian duty to determine the destinies of the much larger non-white majority; members of that majority bitterly resent a situation in which they have no control over their own destiny, no share in decision-making. This is the issue on which everything turns, though economic and social disabilities also play their part.

We tend to speak of Latin America as a unity. In point of fact this is a complex world of twenty independent republics, each with its own history and special characteristics. But there are certain conditions which seem to be general, and a number of problems which are endemic in that area. Nowhere in the world is the gap between affluence and poverty greater, nowhere has peaceful evolution in the direction of justice and equality proved more difficult to achieve. Philip Agee's book *Inside the Company: C.I.A. Diary* (Penguin, 1974) is still too recent to have been critically assessed and checked. But even if no more than ten per cent of what he records is found to be reliable, that is quite enough to show the astonishing ineptitude and folly, to put it no lower, of the American intervention in Latin American countries, and the extent to which the use or misuse of

79

funds from abroad have tended to hinder reform and keep in power corrupt and ineffective forms of government. No wonder that those who sow the wind are in danger of reaping the whirlwind.

Christians have long been aware of these situations and disturbed by them. It is not surprising that those most deeply involved in them have begun to work out their own theologies, in the light of experience and the understanding of the Christian gospel to which such experience has led them.

Black Theology has been developing rapidly in the United States. The term itself is ambiguous. If it means simply that those who have lived under oppression will read the gospels in their own way and will develop insights denied to those who have never shared the experience, this is self-evidently true. Theology always grows out of life. If it emphasizes the fact that for the last thousand years the majority of those who have written theological books have been heirs of a white civilization, this is also true and not without its importance. But if it is understood to mean that the remedy for an alleged White Theology is to substitute for it a Black Theology, it is immediately clear that such a Black Theology will be just as distorted and out of relation to reality as that which it replaces. The extent to which this can be carried can be illustrated from the writings of one of the most articulate of the exponents of Black Theology, Dr. James H. Cone. In his book *Black Theology and Black Power* (Seabury Press), he writes:

> God's word of reconciliation means that we can only be justified by becoming black. Reconciliation makes us all black. Through this radical change, we become identified with the suffering of the black masses. It is this that makes all white churches anti-Christian in their essence. To be Christian is to be one of those whom God has chosen. God has chosen black people.

Such words sound oddly when read in an Indian context. Why should anyone whom God has made brown wish to become black? This is in fact the last thing that any Asian wants. But the absurdity of the language should not conceal from us the sincerity of the writer and his concern with things that really matter. If he had written 'human' instead of 'black', we should understand better what he means. As we have already said, the problem for us all is that of remaining human in a world in which humanity is so widely denied. Our concern must be with the 'human face of God'; and that we cannot recover unless we all recover it together.

Independent theology has not yet made much progress in South Africa, not unnaturally since the government's policy of *apartheid* has deliberately set back the development of the education of the majority; in some ways the black peoples are less advanced than they were at the beginning of the century. But clearly Black Theology imported from the United States has a great appeal for sufferers under the heel of the present régime. A weakness of this theology is that it seems to live in the world of the Old Testament rather than that of the New. The Exodus of Israel from Egypt is taken as the great historic manifestation of God's saving power; with a strong right hand and mighty works he brings his people out of captivity; – not much thought seems yet to have been given to what happens to the people of God when they have crossed the Red Sea and entered into the wilderness. And who is the Messiah? A Black friend of mine who is a member of one of the African independent churches, when asked this question, answered without hesitation, 'Black power is the Messiah'. We remain friends. But I wonder how my friend would answer the question as to the rôle of Jesus Christ in his theology. Are we to be content with Moses as deliverer, or are we called to look beyond him to another Deliverer and to a deliverance of a kind different from that of the Exodus from Egypt?

In Latin America the Roman Catholic Church seemed to be so closely wedded to the *status quo* as to make it unlikely that any theology of liberation would come from that quarter. But (as so often) it is the unexpected which has happened. Thoughtful Roman Catholics have become deeply aware of the extent to which the Church has compromised itself and cut itself off from the possibility of real Christian witness by its identification with the oppressors; they are convinced that the Church must change its entire policy and now stand out boldly on the side of the oppressed. In this connexion the name of Bishop Helder Camara has become widely known. A declaration of Latin American bishops assembled at Medellín in Colombia in 1968 has attracted wide attention.

A good deal of the early writing on this subject was sentimental, confused and superficial. But the theology has developed and taken on more serious and more biblical forms. From the Roman Catholic side the best book so far available in English is probably the work of Fr. G. Gutierrez, *A Theology of Liberation* (Eng. trans. SCM Press, 1973). Fr. Gutierrez does really try to think theologically in the light of existing situations; he carries his thought forward to the centrality of Jesus Christ in God's work for the liberation and the reconciliation of all men to himself. He sees clearly that oppressed and oppressors alike are in need of the grace and favour of God.

This thinking started in the Roman Catholic Church. The Evangelical forces tended to be more conservative and to hold back from involvement in the new ferment of thought. This is no longer the case. English readers now have access to the Protestant reaction to the situation in a most important work recently published by Dr. Jose Miguez Bonino of Buenos Aires, whose election at Nairobi as one of the Presidents of the World Council of Churches was a recognition of his new rôle in the theological world. His book *Liberation Theology Comes of Age* (SPCK, 1975) will undoubtedly be widely read, and deserves to be read. Dr. Bonino, an Argentinian, serves in the Evangelical Faculty of Theology in Buenos Aires; he has studied abroad and is familiar with Protestant theology in a number of languages. He is a somewhat recent convert to the revolutionary cause.

Like other Latin American thinkers, Bonino accepts hook, line and sinker the Marxist analysis of society. He sees Latin American history in three periods. There was the period following on the conquest by Spain and Portugal, in which organization was purely feudal and all power was concentrated in the hands of a small number of landowners. This was modified by the first revolution and the independence of the republics in the early years of the nineteenth century. This was followed by the entry of European entrepreneurs (mainly Protestant and British) who built the railways, started manufactures, introduced modern ideas of education, and incidentally built up rapidly-growing Protestant churches. But the final effect of all this was the creation of a bourgeois élite, which did not effect the liberation of the toiling masses, overworked, underpaid and undernourished. Now has come the third period, in which the masses must take control of their own destinies and by the overthrow of the existing powers bring in a new period of freedom and prosperity. Bonino has no doubt at all that at this point all believing

Christians must take the side of the oppressed; there is no alternative.

Two words appear with great frequency in all the literature of this school, as also in the proceedings of the Assemblies at Bangkok and Nairobi: *humanization* and *conscientization.*

Humanization.[5] The first step is to help people to recover their humanity. Some would go so far as to say that humanization is evangelization; in a situation of oppression there is no other form of the preaching of the gospel. At a certain level of oppression, man loses the human substance; he has been deprived of all that makes the existence of man genuinely human. The first step in recovery is to give him back a sense of his own reality and dignity as a human being.

Conscientization. In English this is a piece of horrible jargon. The invention of the term is usually ascribed to the Latin American writer Paulo Freire,[6] whose work *Pedagogy of the Oppressed* appeared in English translation in 1973 (published by Penguin). The term is doubly unfortunate in English. It has nothing whatever to do with 'conscience' as that word is generally used in English. *Conscience* in French (as in other languages of Latin origin) often means 'consciousness', and that is what is at issue here. Conscientization is only an extremely awkward way of expressing the awakening of consciousness. Fr. Gutierrez well expresses what is meant: 'in this process, the oppressed person rejects the oppressive consciousness which dwells in him, becomes conscious of himself, and finds his own language. He becomes, by himself, less dependent and freer, as he commits himself to the transformation and building up of society'. With much of this the Christian can unconditionally agree. At a certain level of poverty and malnutrition, human faculties become atrophied. Man is hardly aware of his misery; things have always been so, and it seems to him hardly possible that they should be changed. He has to become aware that they can be changed and that he himself has to take a hand in changing them.

[5] The January 1971 edition of the *International Review of Mission* (WCC, 1971) was dedicated to the theme 'Humanization and Mission'.

[6] Freire has himself, in an article in *Cross Currents*, declined the honour of this invention; however, he is certainly responsible for its wide diffusion.

Where the Christian must take issue with this revolutionary theology is in the conviction that humanization and conscientization can be regarded as a substitute for evangelization, the direct preaching of the gospel of Jesus Christ, or that they can rightly precede the preaching of the gospel. Here history is against the revolutionaries.

The Church after all has had a great deal of experience in working among those at the extreme limit of poverty and degradation. In India missionaries found themselves faced by the challenge of the scheduled communities. Desperately poor, illiterate, sunk in habits which made it almost impossible for them to lift themselves up out of misery, these people did not seem to be exactly the material out of which flourishing churches could be built up. There were in fact two views as to the way in which they could be approached. One group held that social reform must precede evangelism; first improve social conditions and then the preaching of the gospel can follow. Others held that from the start the gospel of salvation must be preached. How can humanization be effected except by the direct and loving approach of a human being, in whom the oppressed can see the likeness of the Man Christ Jesus, the One in whom the true nature of human life is seen? How can a man become conscious of his own true being except through acquaintance with the living Christ, the true liberator from everything that mars and distorts the existence of God's children?

The working out of these two views is interesting. Those who started out with the idea of social reform were singularly ineffective in bringing it about, and never got on to the preaching of the gospel. Those who started with a gospel of conversion, perhaps without intending it brought about a social revolution, as believers became liberated from harmful habits and became aware with new self-respect that even under the yoke of oppression many thing in their situation could be changed. It is a simple fact that two members of these oppressed communities are now bishops of the Christian Church. As we have recorded, much still remains to be done in the way of political liberation; what has been accomplished could hardly have come about without the preparatory work of the Christian mission.

To return to Dr. Bonino; he affirms that European theology reflects the bourgeois origin of the theologian, and consequently overlooks many things that are really there in the gospel; such a theologian soft-pedals or altogether overlooks the revolutionary elements that are there in the teaching of Jesus. The Latin American must therefore free himself from the trammels of this theological tradition, and go out on his own in the discovery of the reality of the gospel. With this no Christian thinker is likely to quarrel. Bonino does make one exception in this general condemnation of the European tradition. Professor Jürgen Moltmann, in his first notable work *Theology of Hope* (Eng. trans. SCM Press, 1967), having accepted a generally Marxist position and brought back Christian hope from vague eschatological expectations to an urgent need for the realization of the kingdom of God among men, seemed to those who were beginning to have revolutionary thoughts to share their vision and to be their prophet. Bonino is distressed to find that Moltmann in his second book, *The Crucified God* (Eng. trans. SCM Press, 1973) seems to have receded from his earlier position and to be less confident in his revolutionary theology. He tries to analyse the reasons for this change of attitude.[7]

The cause can be given in a single word: Czechoslovakia. Central Europe is a long way from Latin America. Bonino, like others of his kind, does not seem to have appreciated the extent to which the reputation of the Russians has been destroyed in Europe by the violent action of the invasion of Czechoslovakia, which must have been carefully prepared for months before it took place, and which has given Western Germany a new frontier with Russian-controlled Eastern Europe. The Russians seem to count on the capacity of ordinary people for forgetting. The suppression of the rising in Berlin, the rape of Hungary and the occupation of Czechoslovakia have followed one another at intervals of roughly ten years. That this is no accident of policy is clearly shown by more recent events in Portugal and Angola. In Portugal the attempt to impose upon the country by armed force the dictatorship of a party which had obtained only ten per cent of the votes in the election seems for the moment to have been frustrated, but there is no certainty that similar attempts at aggression will not be made in the future. The shameless neo-colonialism of the attempt in Angola to impose (by the latest and most sophisticated weapons of war) the rule of a minority on an African country newly emerging from its colonial age has

[7] His careful analysis is on pages 144–52 of *Liberation Theology Comes of Age*.

shown up the reality of Russian political aims to all except those who are so imbued with a particular ideology as to be incapable of either thought or observation.

So we cannot evade the question who are the oppressors. Dr. Bonino (if asked) would reply, 'the possessing class'. Almost everyone in Western Europe, on the other hand, would reply, 'The Russians – whatever their pretence of being the liberating and democratic forces'. So easily can the oppressed become the oppressor; so deeply can the love of power enter the hearts of those who profess that their only aim is to help the Lord in putting down the mighty from their seats.

The mind of many sympathetic observers in Europe has been made anxious by the naïve Utopianism of much of this Latin American thinking. The word 'Utopia' went out of common usage in Europe sixty years ago; it has come back with a vengeance into Latin American writing, and also into a number of the documents of the World Council. Naturally, if we want to change society we must have some dreams as to what kind of society we want to produce, and this does no harm if dreams are not confused with realities. Danger comes as soon as we give in to the myth of the sinless proletariat, and suppose that wickedness is always on the side of those whom we identify as the oppressors, and innocence on the side of those whom we commiserate as the oppressed.

The Marxist Utopian dreams, as cited by Dr. Bonino, sound particularly ridiculous in view of what has happened in the last few years; such pictures could much more easily be drawn of Britain than of any country under Marxist control.[8] With all our imperfections we still know what freedom is. When the oppressed Asian is turned out of Kenya or Uganda, where does he turn? His Mecca is Canada. Once admitted he finds himself in a country where there is no colour bar, where a man can find honest work and a good livelihood, where society is singularly

[8] Bonino quotes from a *Handbook of Marxism–Leninism* by Kuusinen such phrases as that the conditions are created 'for an unlimited development of personality and the physical and spiritual fulfilment of man . . . and all of this, far from being a static goal, is an endless march towards glittering peaks of civilization and human development which we can still not even surmise'. Even Bonino is fain to admit that 'it is possible to smile cynically at these predictions'. Surely better than 'cynically' is the word 'realistically'.

tolerant and open. He has exchanged an atmosphere of suspicion and ill will for the breath of freedom. Perhaps there is more to be said for the west than is often allowed in Marxist or ecumenical propaganda.

It all depends on whether you believe in original sin or not. If you believe, as Karl Marx seems to have believed, that evil exists only in circumstances, that man is naturally good and that given a change in social conditions goodness will reassert itself, you will live in the Utopian dream. If you are realistic enough to recognize that evil is present in us all, in revolutionary parties no less than in the hearts of conservatives, you will be content to bargain for far less, not to expect too much and yet to believe that partial gains can be made and human dignity can be promoted. In sixty years Britain has lived through a non-violent revolution; life is far better for the majority of the people than it was two generations ago. Not all has been accomplished and there is still much to be done. But shall we exchange the liberty that we have, in hopes of an even more ample liberty, for what we now know to be the certainty of enslavement?

4. Violence and Non-violence

We have felt it right to indicate some holes in Dr. Bonino's carefully worked-out argument. This must not be taken to mean that we for one moment deny that radical changes are needed in the Latin American situation. But we are entitled to a clear answer to one major question. Many supporters of revolutionary movements hold the view that, when things are as bad as they are in many countries today, no radical change can be hoped for without the use of violence, and that therefore revolutionary violence is a natural activity for Christians.

It is not to be supposed that there is anything new or original in this point of view. Mazzini, the herald of Italian liberation, is generally believed to have held a vaguely Christian view of things, and yet this is precisely the view which he held. Dr. Werner Stark's analysis of his position is illuminating:

This is a genuine messianism borne by a genuine faith. The other messianisms . . . monarchical and republican, ended by glorifying the murderous steel. Needless to say Mazzini's does the same. The war of the herald-people and all the oppressed cannot but be holy. But it is not only the bayonet, weapon of open combat, which

Mazzini . . . praises, it is also the dagger, the weapon of sly assault as well. 'Sacred the sword of Judith!' he cries, 'sacred the arrow of Tell.'[9]

Apart from one single word, the Garibaldian paraphrase of the Lord's prayer might equally well have been written by Che Guevara:

> Thy will be done in barracks as in the field of battle;
> Give us ammunition each day.
> And do not lead us into the temptation of counting the number of the enemy
> But deliver us from the Austrians and the priests.

Dr. Cone, in the work from which we have already quoted, discusses the question of violence and dismisses it as a subordinate and relative question. He quotes from an earlier writing of Dr. Bonino in the following terms:

> It is subordinate because it has to do with the 'cost' of desired change – the question of the legitimacy of revolution is not decided on the basis of the legitimacy of violence and vice versa. Violence is a cost that must be estimated and pondered in relation to a particular revolutionary situation. It is 'relative', because in most revolutionary situations, violence is already a fact constitutive of the situation; injustice, slave labour, hunger and exploitation are forms of violence which must be weighed against the cost of revolutionary violence.[10]

This passage is typical of the harm done to clear thinking by a cloudy and ill-defined use of terms; if all injustice is to be identified with violence, then we shall have to invent an entirely new vocabulary, if we are to think seriously about the problems raised by the situations that we have been discussing. It is clear that, here as elsewhere, much attention needs to be paid to the study of meanings, and that theological attention needs to be paid to the question of violence and non-violence much more accurately than has often been the case in the past.

Some time before the Uppsala Assembly of the World Council held in 1968 the suggestion was made that that Assembly should concentrate on one single theological subject rather than

[9] Werner Stark, *The Sociology of Religion* (Routledge), vol. I, page 197.

[10] *Black Theology and Black Power*, pages 142–43.

dissipate its attention on many; the subject proposed for discussion was precisely that of violence in relation to the commands of Christ. Subsequent history has shown how practical and relevant this suggestion was; nothing in the history of the World Council has been more controversial than the financial support given to organizations committed to the use of violence, though it was asserted by the Council that all money which passed through its hands was earmarked strictly for non-violent purposes. Evidently the subject is still open for impartial debate.

It may clear the air a little to take a look at two areas of the world in which violence has manifested itself naked and unashamed, and to enquire what have so far been the consequences of such violence.

Events in Northern Ireland confirm the view that violence breaks out not when things are at their worst, but when they show signs of becoming better. Terence O'Neill, now Lord O'Neill of the Mayne, as Prime Minister of Northern Ireland was working very quietly to reduce the tensions between his country and the Irish Republic; at that time relations between the two were probably better than they had been at any time since the establishment of the Irish Free State in 1922. But some people did not want relations to get better, they wanted them to get worse. It is unlikely that these mischief-makers foresaw the consequences of their actions; but naturally the so-called Irish Republican Army seized the opportunity, and started a campaign of senseless violence. A study of this ruthless, humourless, unscrupulous campaign is illuminating. The acknowledged aim of it is to make the territory ungovernable. What has come out of it? What has been the result of the deaths of more than a thousand innocent people? The answer is that violence has proved wholly counter-productive. Forty years ago thoughtful Ulstermen such as my uncles were saying, 'We've got to unite with them sooner or later; we had better start making the plans now'. If asked 'When do you expect union to be achieved?' they would answer 'In about twenty-five years'. Asked the same question after the withdrawal of Ireland from the Commonwealth and the establishment of the Republic, they would have replied, 'Not for a very long time; perhaps a thousand years'. If the same question is posed today, the unhesitating answer is 'Never'. 'Never' is a big word; it is possible that the Protestants of Ulster could be wrong. But that is the net result to date of the campaign of violence carried out by the IRA.

The situation in Cyprus, with its mixed population of Greeks and Turks, had been uneasy ever since the occupation of the island by Britain in 1878. But there had never been anything like a systematic campaign of terrorism. This began when the Greeks raised the cry of *Enosis* – union with Greece – and brought in 'General Grivas' to start a terrorist campaign against the British. The Turks made it perfectly plain to the British foreign minister that, if the campaign for *Enosis* persisted they would invade and occupy the island. The result was the agreement that Cyprus should be independent within the British Commonwealth, the agreement being guaranteed by Britain, Greece and Turkey. The plans for invasion were not abandoned but for the time being put in cold storage. In 1974 the cry of *Enosis* was again raised by hot-headed Greek officers brought in to train Cypriot troops. The Turks immediately did what they had all along told the world they would do, invading Cyprus, expelling 200,000 Greek Cypriots from their home and occupying forty per cent of the land surface of the island. At the time of writing there is no sign that they intend ever to yield an inch of what they have taken over. Once again violence is seen to have been completely counter-productive. Violence on one side has led to successful counter-violence on the other, and has divided 'for ever' an island which can prosper only if it is united.

These facts ought to be carefully considered by those who regard violence as offering a solution in situations of tension or oppression.

What ought to be the attitude of Christians in such situations? There appear to be three possible points of view.

1. Some Christians hold that, in a situation of oppression, violence is a natural and necessary form of Christian activity. If we hold that a transfer of power is absolutely necessary, and agree with Chairman Mao that power comes out of the barrel of a gun, the conclusion would seem to follow logically: violence is justified, indeed necessary, when the aim to which it is directed is approved by the conscience of the one who takes this stance. It is then easy to see how it was possible for Che Guevara to maintain that the heart of the revolutionary must be filled with love for the opponent, even when he is engaged in the revolution-

ary task of shooting him down. He was not the first to think that every man kills that which he loves.

2. The situation is far less simple for those who hold that violence is always evil, but that situations may arise in which violence is the lesser of two evils. This was the dilemma faced by the large number of Christians who between the two world wars had come very near to a pacifist position, but with the rise of Hitler found it necessary to review the conclusions that they had reached and the premises on which those conclusions had been based. If it is taken for granted that war is the worst of all evils, then the conclusion is quite clear; any participation by a Christian in the kind of violence represented by war is a betrayal of the gospel. But what if it should appear that there are evils worse than war? This was the dilemma faced by my generation. The pacifist tends to see the choice in simplified terms: 'If you are not a pacifist, that means that you approve of war as an instrument of policy.' He has not even begun to understand the dilemma. If the choice is between having on your hands the blood of your friends, or the blood of those whom you judge to be enemies of the human race, what do you do? It was still worse for those in Germany, who had to decide whether in the circumstances the assassination of Hitler could be defended. Dietrich Bonhoeffer was the best known of those who wrestled in agony with this question. It is usually the man in the middle who makes the worst of both worlds.

3. Many Christians hold that the following of Christ implies the total rejection of violence and the refusal in any way to participate in violent action. This is no new position in the Christian world. The peace churches, of which the best known is the Society of Friends, have steadfastly maintained it and thereby constituted themselves a challenge to the rest of the Christian world.

But our contemporary advocates of violence maintain that this is in reality no option at all. To quote once again from James Cone—

If he decides to take the 'non-violent' way, then he is saying that revolutionary violence is more detrimental to men in the long run than systemic violence.[11]

---

[11] op. cit., page 143. But why the inverted commas? Non-violence

The point deserves consideration. The terms 'established violence' and 'structured violence' have become part of the ecumenical jargon, being directed against régimes of which those who use the terms happen to disapprove.

It is a fact that there are degrees of support for the doctrine of non-violence. Few except the anarchists would deny the advantages of having a police force. It is generally agreed that, if violence breaks out in a country, the state has the right and duty to bring violence under control and if necessary to suppress it by violent means. In this sense every state is a form of established violence. Even Switzerland, that peaceful country which is perhaps the most civilized area on the face of the earth, and the amenities of which the World Council has enjoyed for so many years, has an armed police which in certain circumstances of disorder would not hesitate to make use of its arms. Karl Marx believed that with the coming of the revolution and the socialist society the state would quietly wither away. Fifty-nine years have passed since the Russian Revolution; so far the state shows no signs at all of withering away. The ruthless form of state capitalism which claims total control over the possessions, the lives and even the thoughts of its citizens bears little resemblance to the hopes of Marx. Christians, tougher and more realistic than Karl Marx, have always recognized the element of sheer evil in human nature as they have known it in themselves and others. They have no Utopian dreams, and recognize that the state, understood by Martin Luther as appointed by God as a barrier against sin, will have to continue to exist until the end of time and the kingdom of God comes with power.

Nevertheless, all Christians agree that that is the best state in which there is least evidence of its coercive power. It is the business of the policeman to make himself invisible. It should be possible for the ordinary citizen to go on his ways in peace, hardly aware of the existence of the state, except of course on the painful day on which he has to calculate his income tax. In the kingdom of God there will be neither coercion nor violence. It is the aim of the Christian that the imperfect society in which he lives should approximate as nearly as possible to the blessed-

---

is a perfectly familiar term in contemporary English. The aim seems simply to be to introduce prejudice into an argument which should be dispassionately conducted.

ness of the kingdom of God. Of course there will always be disagreement among Christians as to how this aim is to be attained. Perfect agreement, like perfect peace, is not one of the prerogatives granted to pilgrims upon this earth.

We may, however, hope to agree as to what it is that we are talking about. What does the word 'violence' mean? Unless we agree on this we are not likely to be able to advance further in discussion.

Violence involves the exercise of constraint upon a human person to ensure that he does what of his own volition he does not wish to do, that he accepts a situation in which he does not wish to be, or that he endures loss or suffering to which he has not himself consented. Here we all agree. It is when the abstract terms are translated into particular, concrete situations that disagreements begin to arise.

It is widely believed, especially in the United States, that Mahatma Gandhi in South Africa and later in India, by his use of non-violent non-co-operation and passive disobedience, introduced into the world an entirely new and better method of political action. Is it clear that the facts justify such an assertion? One of our great needs is a reliable biography of Gandhi and a critical assessment of his words and deeds, something which as yet has hardly been attempted. He himself maintained that his only aim was to bring his opponents to a better mind, so that they would wish to do what Gandhi himself felt it right that they should do. But is this a complete account of his methods and actions? Did the actions of his followers correspond to his intentions and the teaching that he had given?

During the non-violent campaigns in India, it was common form for students to lie down on railway tracks to prevent the trains from running. They quite sincerely believed that their action was a purely non-violent protest, but that if the police came and picked them up and carried them off out of harm's way, this was a manifestation of brutal violence. They had adopted the over-simplified view of violence which identifies it simply with the use of physical force. But this will not do. Violence, as we have defined it, is a much more complex business than the mere application of *force majeure*.

The word 'boycott' has become part of the English language. It is sometimes forgotten that, in the actions taken against the unfortunate Captain Boycott in 1880, not a finger was lifted against him; all that was done was to withdraw from every kind of contact with him, and to withhold every kind of service. The aim, successfully carried out, was simply to make it impossible for him to survive in the area for which he was responsible.[12] It must be recognized that any form of attack against the pocket, the comfort or the reputation of any individual partakes of the nature of violence, even when it is maintained that the aim of the action is ultimately to do him good and not harm. Every industrial strike is of its nature violent, even though no physical action is involved. Its aim is either to bankrupt the employer, if he will not concede what he does not wish to concede, or to harass the public to the point at which so much inconvenience will be caused as to ensure that the pressure of public opinion will be brought to bear on the employer until he gives way. This may be held to be justifiable violence, but it is violence none the less. Karl Marx was more honest than some of his followers; he spoke plainly in terms of class war – and war is usually admitted to be a violent method of procedure.

No one can read contemporary ecumenical literature without realizing how much confusion there is on this subject, both in language and consequently in thought. The most eminent disciple of Mahatma Gandhi in recent times was Martin Luther King. No doubt King intended his actions to be non-violent. Did he carry out his intentions to the end? When he said, 'If we cannot persuade you by our words, we will persuade you by our deeds', what did the word 'persuade' mean? Had he crossed over the narrow boundary between genuine non-violence and non-violence in which there is actually concealed violence?

I am not attempting to answer that question. I am simply pleading for a more careful use of language as a preliminary to more careful theological thinking in this whole area of confusion. Not long ago a leading African Christian was quoted as having adduced in a sermon the use that God made of the violence inflicted on Jesus Christ in the crucifixion to effect the salvation of mankind, as a justification for the violent methods adopted by men in certain situations to effect their own liberation from oppression. When language is used (or misused) in

[12] See the *Encyclopaedia Britannica* s.v. Boycott: 'undoubtedly an illegal conspiracy to injure the person, property or business of another by unwarrantably putting pressure on all and sundry to withdraw from him their business or social intercourse'.

such a fashion, communication becomes impossible. The only remedy is more careful definition of the terms that we use, careful theological study of Holy Scripture, agreement as to the nature of the salvation about which we are talking, and the rejection of speaking and thinking which do not stand up to the test of careful and accurate analysis. Perhaps the linguistic analysts have some ground for their criticism of the sloppiness of Christians in their use of words, their confusion in the application of intellectual concepts and their disingenuousness in the manipulation of both terms and ideas to suit their own preconceptions.

We may end this section with a protest against an attitude which is all too commonly taken up by the advocates or defenders of violence. Many Christians take the view that persuasion is the only weapon that God has put into the hands of the believers in Jesus Christ. Those who hold that other weapons are legitimate constantly stigmatize this attitude as involving passive acquiescence in the *status quo*, or even a conditional approval of it. This seems to rest upon a simplistic division of the world into oppressors and oppressed. It would be difficult to count the number of times that the word 'oppression' occurred in the documents of the Nairobi Assembly. The challenge is often put in the terms, 'If you are not unconditionally on the side of the oppressed, you are necessarily an oppressor'. This assumes that it is easy in the world today to determine clearly who are the oppressors and who are the oppressed; and also to conclude not only that the oppressed are right in their desire for liberation but also that they are justified in all the methods they adopt with a view to the achievement of their aims.

The Christian belief in persuasion is in fact a highly dynamic point of view. It is realistic in that it works in terms of situations as they actually are, and not as wishful thinking would have them to be. It is reasonable in that it works in terms of possibilities and not in the categories of Utopian euphoria. It is prophetic in that it looks beyond the immediate future. It is constructive in that it believes in laying foundations which will stand the test of time. Above all it is based on a biblical understanding of good and evil, and of the will of God as revealed in Jesus Christ. It accepts the obligation of unconditional obedience to him and recognition of the hard reality that obedience to

95

the One who endured the cross for our redemption will involve participation in his sufferings as well as in his resurrection.

5. The End of It All

Ecumenical debates over the last twenty years have revealed deep divisions among Christians as to the courses of action that may be adopted by Christians in the perplexing situations which confront us today. It is not the case that these divisions can be readily or easily resolved. What *is* possible is to recognize that these divisions occur within a context of wide agreement on fundamental issues. This is not to deny the reality of the divisions. But, in the occasional acerbities of debate, the realities of agreement are sometimes lost from view. It may not be without value to attempt to identify the nature and extent of these agreements.

1. All Christians are agreed that oppression of one human being by another is always an evil thing. Authority, with the corresponding implication of a measure of subordination, will always play a part in human affairs. Otherwise any kind of ordered existence becomes impossible. But the moment that authority disregards the personal dignity of the one who is expected to obey, it becomes oppressive. More than two thousand years ago the Greek tragedian Euripides declared that slavery takes away half a man's manhood from him. The general opinion of mankind today is that slavery is intolerable, since it infringes the principle that no man may ever be used simply as an instrument for the fulfilment of another's purposes. But this holds true of every form of economic exploitation, of the suppression of the right of a minority to express its views and live its own life within the limits of public order, of the tyranny of majorities over minorities or of minorities over majorities, of indoctrination and brain-washing, of the withholding or distortion of information, and of all the other means by which the human substance is diminished and the image of God defaced.

2. 'Humanization' is therefore a laudable aim. There are situations in which human dignity cannot be fully restored without extensive changes in the social and political order. But humanization can begin long before such changes can be

regarded as possible or likely. There is no situation of alienation or degradation in which man cannot begin to become aware of his dignity as a child of God. The Christian takes the view that the most powerful force of all on the side of humanization is the love of God revealed in Jesus Christ, and that this can best come home to those who need it through the love of a human friend for those who have never known before what it means to be unconditionally loved.

3. Oppressed and oppressors alike are children of God. Each needs the restoration of the image of God which has been defaced in each, though in different ways. Evil is a great power in human affairs. It is not the case that evil is all on the side of the oppressors, and virtue in pure form only on the side of the oppressed. Hatred can beget nothing but hatred. Selfishness and ambition are mixed up with more admirable motives in almost all human action. The Christian must therefore maintain a certain attitude of detachment and criticism, even in relation to causes in which he is whole-heartedly engaged. Utopianism cannot be part of any genuinely Christian programme.

4. It follows that evangelization must accompany and not follow every step in the process of political and economic liberation. All the time we are all under the judgement of God. Those who aim at bringing in the kingdom of God may bring in a reasonably tolerable kingdom of man. Those who aim only at bringing in the kingdom of man are much more likely to produce a very fair imitation of the kingdom of the devil. This is not to affirm the kind of pessimism which paralyses action; it is to claim that, since the purposes of God are always wider than the concerns of men, any enterprise on which we desire to invoke the blessing of God must be consciously and deliberately brought into conformity with his will of good for all men and must be continuously submitted to his judgement. All the time we are under judgement as well as under grace.

5. One of our greatest needs is for accurate information as to what is going on in the world. But this is just what is difficult to come by in our days. The media to a large extent have become instruments of propaganda and not servants of the truth. Anyone who has lived in the South African Republic (and not merely visited it) knows how complicated that situation is, and how

different his experiences are from the kind of information which the mass media make available.

Several Christian sources of information on the affairs of the world do exist. It has to be admitted with regret that some, though of course not all, of the secular sources are better informed, more complete and more reliable than those provided by the Christian churches. Here is a field in which ecumenical co-operation might produce results far better than those which so far have been attained. All of us need all the help we can get towards the formation of an educated Christian judgement on all the perplexing situations by which we are confronted in the modern world.

6. If Christians take the view (as many do) that persuasion is the ultimate, or indeed the only Christian weapon in the campaign to put things right when they are wrong, such Christians are called upon to carry on a steady unremitting campaign for the development of responsible public opinion far beyond the limits of the Christian world. In many cases all that is needed is the publication of the facts without note or comment. Most governments are highly sensitive to world opinion. Violence usually has the result of hardening them in their own self-righteousness. The temperate statement of undeniable fact can lead sometimes with surprising rapidity to the remedying of injustice.

7. Christian attitudes towards situations of crisis have always varied and vary today. It is unlikely that either side will in the near future persuade the other of the rightness of its position. What is needed is a little mutual forbearance and tolerance, the avoidance of abusive terms in either direction, willingness to listen and a readiness to believe that one has not perfectly understood the position taken up by fellow-Christians. After all, both share one common concern – the establishment of righteousness upon earth as a sign of the present reality of the kingdom of God.

8. All are agreed, or should be, that in situations of crisis the only real service is to be there. When Garibaldi was raising the standard of liberty in Italy, his ranks were joined by young idealists from many countries at peril of their lives. While my own view is that the young men from many countries who during the civil war in Spain fought on the communist side were

gravely mistaken in their judgement of the political situation, no one could withhold admiration for the spirit in which they went to give their lives.

In the modern world some governments have made it impossible 'to be there'. In other areas, such as South Africa, it is possible 'to be there' provided that certain conditions are fulfilled. Nothing is gained if the Christian crusader acts in such a way as to ensure his deportation before his ministry has even begun. Yet to sit still, to observe, to become aware of the realities of the situation before taking any action – such things make heavy demands on one's patience, especially that of the young. In such patience there is bound to be suffering; but was there ever any following of the crucified Christ which did not involve suffering?

'Let us endure an hour and see injustice done.' These words of the poet A. E. Housman could be no more than the expression of a rueful cynicism. But they can be understood also in terms of Christian wisdom. Is it better to stay in a painful situation and to suffer, or to run away from the painful situation? Perhaps after all the really important thing is just to be there. To maintain a quiet, resolute, persistent, courteous opposition to every form of evil is never an easy task. But in the end it is the most effective method, and the one least productive of evil in response to evil. It is the constant dropping of water that in the end wears away the stone.

5

TRAINING – FOR WHAT?

There was a time when the Church had a monopoly of education, and therefore had almost complete control over the minds of the Christian people and the coming generation. That time is now at an end. In a number of countries the Church is altogether excluded from the educational process, in some to the extent that it is not able to give any formal education at all to young people. In others the position of the Church has become marginal and, though it may be able to give what is called religious education, the formation of educational policies as a whole is no longer within its sphere. But education is of so great an importance in the life of men that the Church cannot abandon its concern for it without ceasing altogether to be the Church.

It is good that one section at Nairobi 1975 occupied itself exclusively with the problems of education. So immense a subject cannot be dealt with in a single chapter of a book like this. It has seemed better to confine this chapter to the one subject of theological education in the broad sense of the term. One sub-section at Nairobi did report on this subject, and found itself highly critical of a great deal of theological education as it is practised in the churches at the present time. But at some points the subsection seemed to show itself unaware of what is really happening in the churches, and to have put forward criticisms that themselves can be made legitimately the target of criticism.

1. A Cry of Distress

Our comments may start appropriately with a cry of distress from West Irian, a distant land with which most of us have but little acquaintance, but in which about half the population is now Christian:

> Take for instance this leadership training centre that has just been built. The whole thing was concocted in Djakarta, and I am afraid

the people who started this know nothing about lay training in Irian Jaya. Sure, the local church wanted it, but they did not know what a white elephant they were receiving as a present. The centre is a group of beautiful brick buildings surrounded by fields cleared of roots and stones. It is intended for people from the villages, people who never lived in a house built of bricks. For them it will be like going to a foreign country. What will they do when they go back to their thatch huts, and poor and thorny land, with all the theory that they have learned here? Then there is the problem of transportation. These people have to be flown in, and we have only small aeroplanes already overworked . . . If we had really thought of the needs of the people, the best thing, probably, would have been to send a team to the villages to spend two or three months with the people there. And then we wouldn't need these buildings.[1]

'Concocted' . . . 'If we had really thought'. In those six words we can read almost the whole of what has gone wrong with the training of men and women for the service of the churches in the third world, and not by any means in the third world alone.

Almost from the beginning of the modern missionary enterprise, wise men had seen that the work of evangelism and of the building up of the Church in non-Christian countries could not be well done until it was done by 'natives', a word which in those days had no derogatory connotations. This was the thought in the minds of William Carey and his colleagues, as they launched the noble enterprise of their College at Serampore,[2] no less in the mind of Bishop Middleton of Calcutta, as he brooded over his grandiose plans for Bishop's College in that city. In each case the plans proved premature. There was no existing church from which an adequate number of students could be drawn and to which they would return. Almost a century was to pass before the colleges could take the lead in the training of ministers for the churches in India and beyond.

In other areas very different plans were followed with success. Much less weight was given to academic attainments, much more to knowledge of the world and experience within the church.

[1] *International Review of Mission*, July 1974, page 375. Note that the planning in Djakarta was carried out by Indonesians and not by foreigners from the west.

[2] See W. S. Stewart, *The Story of Serampore and its College* (Serampore, n.d.). The prospectus of the College is dated July 18, 1818.

101

The presence of Bishop Hannington in Mombasa in 1885, on his way to a martyr's death in Uganda, made possible the first ordination of African clergymen in that area. The two chosen for this vocation (a third had died before the arrival of the bishop) were 'Nasik boys', Africans who had been carried off into slavery by Arabs, rescued by British gunboats, dumped in western India, and rescued a second time by devout missionaries of the Church Missionary Society. These cared for them, trained them as Christians and prepared them for life in the world. A number of these men returned to East Africa. Some found service with David Livingstone. This explains how it came about that, when he died in 1873, at his first funeral the Anglican Burial service was read over him in English. Others stayed at the coast and became faithful helpers of the missionaries in the early and difficult days of the mission. Long experience and faithful service were reckoned as adequate substitutes for formal academic training.

As the Church in Uganda began to grow beyond the power of the missionaries to render all the services that were needed, the wise Bishop Tucker began to ordain to the ministry men in middle life who had given evidence of powers of leadership in the life of the community, and who in some cases were actually hereditary chiefs. Personal merit and social status were relied on to offset the drawbacks of limited theological knowledge. Perhaps the last of the notable men of this lineage was Canon Apolo Kivebulaya, to whom we have already referred as the pioneer missionary in the rain forest of the Congo. His great friend Dr. A. F. Schofield, to whom we owe many of the delightful photographs with which the biography of the saint is adorned,[3] once remarked to me: 'Of course, the old man was practically illiterate, you know'. Deep friendship and respect made this exaggeration permissible; as a matter of fact Apolo knew Swahili quite well, though his knowledge of English was limited and his knowledge of technical theology hardly existed. His immense influence was due to qualities other than those which are learned in a theological college.

The real conflict in Africa in recent years has been that between the old African aristocracy of position and inherited dig-

---

[3] Anne Luck, *African Saint: the Story of Apolo Kivebulaya* (London, 1963).

nity, and the new aristocracy of the book. The Church has not been exempt from the tensions arising from this conflict.

When in 1846 the great battle on behalf of a village ministry in South India had been fought and won, it was agreed to take the best of the village catechists, men of tried and true character who might not know a word of English, give them a thorough training in their own language in biblical knowledge, Christian doctrine and pastoral work, and then ask the bishops to ordain them to work under the direction of a missionary in a rapidly growing village church. The intellectual capacity of these men should not be underestimated. It is now permissible to reveal that at the Lambeth Conference of Anglican bishops held in 1948, when the subject of church union in South India was being discussed and some of the bishops were moaning and groaning about the way in which simple and ignorant Indian Christians were being led astray by western missionaries, I brought the house down by informing the bishops present that Bishop Butler's *Analogy of Religion* had been translated into Tamil in 1858 and published in monthly parts for the edification of the village workers of that date. I did not enquire how many of their lordships had read that celebrated work. Nevertheless, these Tinnevelly clergy of more than a century ago were chosen not primarily on the score of intelligence but rather on the basis of spiritual maturity and reliability. They had grown up among the people to whom they were to minister and knew their needs as no missionary and no city-dwelling Indian could know them. Many of them knew no language other than their own, but in that language could express themselves readily and to the point. Though not learned, they were better educated than those whom they served; and they were ordained at an age and with a measure of experience which would carry weight with the village people.

So matters went on in many areas for many years. But situations change and methods must change with them. One of the achievements of the Council of Trent had been the formation of seminaries, professional institutions for the training of the ordained ministry and for nothing else. The separation of Church and state in America led almost inevitably to the segregation of theology from other academic disciplines. The missionary societies tended to follow suit. Theological schools and seminaries came into existence in every part of the world in isolation from the rest of the educational process, and all too often in places remote from the life of the churches which the students were being trained to serve.

2. Dangerous Places

Seminaries may be a necessary part of the apparatus of the churches. It can hardly be denied that they are dangerous places.

Some are undenominational. These generally have the advantage of a stronger teaching staff and of better financial support than the denominational institutions. But it is not long before the question forces itself upon the attention as to precisely why these students are being trained. Training for the ministry cannot be carried out in the abstract. It is always training related to the ministry of one particular church. In our present divided state churches have differing standards of doctrine and a whole variety of liturgical traditions. They differ also in their understanding of the nature of the ministry, and in their expectations as to the kind of service that the ordained minister should be able to render in the church. How can a minister be effectively trained if no particular form of ministry is in view? Where is it supposed that he will be able to gain the specific knowledge that he will need in the situation in which he is being sent to serve?

Apprised of these difficulties, some churches have steadily refused to be lured into any united efforts and have maintained the independence of their own denominational institutions. Having escaped the jaws of Scylla, they immediately fall victim to Charybdis. Unless the teachers are men of exceptionally broad outlook, the perils of narrowness can hardly be avoided. A certain denominational slant is likely to find its way into the teaching of almost every subject. A fixed and familiar liturgical pattern has great advantages; yet, if it is followed too closely, students will remain unaware of much that is happening in other Churches and perhaps even in their own Church in other areas. A member of a religious order, sent out to look at a seminary which the order was thinking of taking over, remarked to the principal, 'You do not seem to have many new books in the library'. He was probably more astonished than he should have been at the reply: 'Why have new books? The old are better'.

These problems are common to seminaries all over the world.

They are compounded with others in the life of churches which have no long Christian tradition behind them.

The first and most serious problem is that of language. In the majority of third-world seminaries the language of instruction is one that none of the students uses as his own. For this there are two reasons. In many areas (other than the Far East) there is no language which can be regarded as the common language of the students. It has seemed natural to turn to one of the languages of the Christian west as the medium of instruction. Then there is the further problem of the accessibility of knowledge. In local languages Christian literature is slowly being produced and the poverty is not quite as grave as it was fifty years ago. But even so, what is available in these languages is minimal as compared to the wealth of Christian literature in any one of the languages of the west. Even seminaries which do use a local language for purposes of instruction have found it necessary to make sure that their students can read English or French or Spanish readily and without difficulty, and thus have the key to a world of knowledge which would otherwise be closed to them.

Once again, it is a question of balancing profit and loss. The gain is immense as regards the field of available knowledge. But what has the student really gained if he has never learnt to think theologically in his own language? If he is not prepared to undergo the extremely hard discipline of thinking back into his own language and its idiom all that he has learnt, only two roads seem to be open to him. Either he preaches as though he had never been to a theological college at all, using the same limited vocabulary and range of ideas as are accessible to the village catechist; or he writes out his sermon in the western language used in the seminary, and then translates it laboriously with the help of a dictionary into the language he used as a child; it cannot be guaranteed that the result will be either lucid or edifying. For years I have been pleading that in these foreign-language seminaries, one Bible paper each year should be taken in the language which the student spoke at home. This will make sure that he maintains at least a partial familiarity with the Bible from which later on he will be preaching, and may even learn to prepare himself to be a reviser of a version which with the help of his knowledge of Greek he may have discovered to be seriously defective. The questions can be set in English and be the same for all candidates. It will never be impossible to find

105

someone capable of marking the paper written in the local language. No attention, as far as I know, has been paid to my suggestion.

Language is only the beginning of our problems. Almost everywhere in the world the approach to theology is purely western. If seminaries are Roman Catholic, the influence of Thomas Aquinas is likely still to be felt, though with less exclusive dominance than a few years ago. In the Anglican world some Platonic influence may have worked its way in through the great theologians of the nineteenth century. Luther transmitted by way of Ferdinand Christian Baur and Rudolf Bultmann is the voice heard in many Lutheran seminaries. The prevailing influence of John Calvin and the Westminster Confession led Dr. Robin Boyd to give to a recently published book the title *India and the Latin Captivity of the Church* (Cambridge University Press, 1974).

What has all this to do with a candidate for the ministry whose grandfather knew nothing of Christianity, and whose godly Christian parents brought him up in a home in which the proudest possession and the only book was a copy of the New Testament in a local language? The west has built up over the centuries a culture that is critical and analytic. This has little to do with the natural way of thinking of the student or with the kind of education that he has received before coming to the seminary. To a large extent the teacher finds himself providing answers to questions that have never been asked, and pouring western medicine down throats that have never been prepared to receive it.

Does this mean that western critical knowledge should be withheld from students in the third world? This would be unreasonable even if it were possible. The objection is not so much to what is taught as to the method by which it is often taught. Anyone can learn up quickly the results of critical enquiry. But educationally nothing could be more harmful than the acquisition of such results without awareness of critical method and of the slow accumulation of knowledge through which the west has learnt to look on the Bible and theology with new eyes. What matters is not the amount of sheer knowledge imparted, but the transformation of the processes of thought without which a genuinely critical approach to knowledge cannot be acquired.

106

Once again we are hampered by the load of western techniques burdened with which we go to our appointed sphere of work. When I started to teach theology in India forty-five years ago, I thought that the first thing necessary was to have a syllabus. So I sat down and worked out a beautiful syllabus for a three-year course of study. Looking back, I can see that my syllabus was purely western, though it did make provision, unlike its predecessors, for the study of Indian religions and of Tamil, the language of the students; I wonder now how it was possible to be so stupid after six years' experience as a missionary. Many years later, a highly intelligent young colleague who was to start a pastors' school in Africa, came to consult me as to how he should run it. My first advice to him was not to have a syllabus; let him have a few clear starting-points but no idea where he was going to end up. I said to him, 'If in the course of a year you get as far as Genesis chapter 12, discussing everything with your students as you go, you will probably have done a far better job than if you had dictated in the same period elementary notes on all the five books of Moses'. All too often it is the tyranny of our western-type syllabus that prevents us from developing in our students enquiring minds and showing them how to acquire for themselves the kind of knowledge that will really be relevant to their needs.

Few of those whom we teach will follow an academic career. What are they going to do with all the academic lumber with which we have filled their mental store-houses? Some will wish to show off their new-found learning and will perplex their hearers with ideas that have nothing to do with their condition. Others, perhaps more sensible, will abandon the whole apparatus, lock, stock and barrel, and devote themselves to more useful pursuits. Few indeed are those who, fired by a deep love of learning, will use their academic training as the foundation on which to build a fuller knowledge of the word of God and of theology as it is relevant to the needs of the people whom they serve.

Since 1938, when the Tambaram Conference declared theological education, with the possible exception of Christian literature, to be the most neglected area in the whole missionary enterprise, serious attempts have been made to remedy some of the glaring defects in the situation. In 1958, through the co-operation of American finance with missionary effort, the

Theological Education Fund (TEF) was brought into being. The Fund has achieved notable results in certain directions, especially in the field of library facilities. When I first inspected the theological school at Limuru in Kenya, in 1950 still a purely Anglican institution, the library contained about a thousand volumes, largely gifts from kind missionaries, who on leaving the country had left behind as a gift to the college the volumes which they regarded as unworthy of transportation to England or America. I advised the Principal to dig a large hole in the ground, and to bury about one third of the books since they seemed to me not merely antiquated but potentially harmful to students who would have to live in the twentieth and not in the nineteenth century. Today there is at Limuru an excellent building, planned to serve as a reading room and not only as a receptacle for books. The number of books has greatly increased and today I would probably not judge more than ten per cent of them as deserving a permanent home in the graveyard.

But – and there are many buts. Twenty-five years ago the college at Limuru had been deliberately planned to resemble an African village. The students were required to spend a certain number of hours every week doing agricultural work on the estate. Every attempt was made to keep them in touch with the kind of village life from which they had come and to which the great majority of them would return after ordination. Today, influenced by the standards which the TEF requires, Limuru is much less like an African village than it was. The students become accustomed to more sophisticated standards of living, and this may not help them in the kind of work to which they have to go.

The increase in the number of books is greatly to be welcomed. But practically all of these are western books. The production of theology in the third-world churches is still pathetically thin. Those who are writing have for the most part been so thoroughly westernized by the training they have received that it is difficult for them to speak with an authentically non-western accent. Even after all these years, Limuru has only one African tutor. Of the foreign tutors, several have had no experience of serving in an African church, having been plunged straight into theological teaching on arrival. Few can speak any African language. Textbooks planned by the TEF are beginning to arrive on the scene; but these are mostly from the pens of western writers. There is still very much to be done.

I sometimes wonder whether we were not doing a better job in India forty years ago. Then the greater part of the teaching was given in Tamil, though the students were well able to use English as a reading language. The chapel was the centre of the life of the college; almost all the worship was in Tamil, and special attention was given to the needs of wives and children and servants. Every student was at work two days in the week in one of the neighbouring Christian villages, and this pastoral work was carefully supervised and discussed. When funds permitted, students went to student camps to pay visits to other seminaries, to see rural reconstruction work and so on. We were and felt ourselves to be a part of the life of the Church. Everything was in context.[4]

The great cry in these days is for the contextualization of theological education.[5] But there would be no need to contextualize unless we ourselves had first taken theological education out of context. Isolation has always been the danger of seminaries. When to geographical and psychological isolation from the general life of the Church are added isolation of language, thought-forms, patterns of thinking, life-style (as we have learnt to call it), that isolation is grievous indeed. How is the evil to be remedied? Certainly not by adding to an already overloaded curriculum one or two extra courses in contemporary history or political orientation, or whatever catchword may be fashionable at the moment. What is needed is radical re-thinking as to what the purpose of a seminary is, and then careful consideration of possible changes and possible alternatives.

A seminary, as an instrument of the life of the Church, must be (if it is to deserve the name) a place of adoration, of fellowship and of proclamation. It may be thought that such a definition overlooks the obvious fact that a seminary must be a place

[4] Lest it be thought that academic standards were neglected, I ought to add that eleven students went on to take in English under their own steam the B.D. degree of Serampore, to which one of them later added the Calcutta degree of M.A. in philosophy.

[5] Till lately I thought that contextualization was the worst of the ecumenical barbarisms by which the English language has of late been debased. I had not at that time heard of conscientization, which now holds the record.

for serious study. But this is far from being the case. No man can preach unless he has learned to wrestle on his knees with the word of the living God, and until the great words of Scripture have so fashioned themselves as parts of his being that they become to him the natural vehicle for his prayer and praise. The process of lecturing and being lectured is, I suppose, inescapable. But unless the teachers are themselves humble learners, they will never be able to make plain to students what it means to be learners in the school of Christ. How will the students ever learn to proclaim the gospel, unless they have been accustomed to hear those whom they revere as friends and teachers, proclaiming to them from the depths of their own experience the unsearchable riches of Christ? Can a seminary be a seminary unless it is perfectly natural for teachers and taught to pray together as individuals and in groups, in addition to the regular liturgical worship of the chapel?

It is by standards such as these that a visiting team should assess the life of a seminary and judge of the value of its life and work to the Church. I will add one thing more. A seminary is not doing its job, unless it produces each year one work of theological significance, either in a local language, or in such form that it is readily susceptible of translation into a local language.

3. No Other Road?

Seminaries and theological colleges play such a large part in the theological scene in the third world that it has been natural to devote a good deal of time and space to them. But it seems clear that, for financial reasons if for no other, extensive reconsideration has to be given to the methods that have been followed in the past, and that experiments of various kinds may have to be tried out as alternatives, or as supplements to the existing forms of training.

The European tradition is that theological education should be given primarily in a university, and that the theological student should in no way be isolated from those studying in other faculties. Even in so recently formed a university as that of Hamburg, and in some of even more recent foundation, it has been taken for granted that the Faculty of Theology is the primary and essential faculty. It stands first in the list in the university handbook. Clearly such an arrangement can be maintained only with difficulty where a large variety of denominations has to be dealt with; indeed in Hamburg itself there is a separate seminary for the training of Baptist ministers. In most countries of the third world, for obvious reasons, the presence of theology in a university is unthinkable. It is, however, the case that in the University of Durban-Westville (the university which serves the Indian community in South Africa) there is both a department of the science of religion and a department of Christian theology (and in fairness be it added, a department of Indology and one of Islamic studies). Where such an arrangement is practicable the advantages are self-evident. Theological students are not segregated from others, and may find themselves in the position of having to stand up for their faith in a less than favourable atmosphere. They are likely to need some specialized denominational training as well; but the greater part of their theological studies will have been carried out in a genuinely academic atmosphere.

Of greater interest in the areas with which we are specially concerned in this chapter is the rapid development of departments of religion in secular universities. This was thought to be impossible in state-supported institutions in the United States, where the separation of Church and state is so strongly insisted on. But even there and even in state universities such departments have been founded and flourish. A number of the younger theologians feel that that is the place to be, at the growing edge of thought and without the sometimes irritating limitations on academic freedom which are encountered in denominational seminaries. A surprising number of the newer universities in the United Kingdom are provided with such facilities. The number of students taking advantage of the possibility of studying religion without prior commitment to any one form of faith shows that religion is very far from being a dead option in the west. It is in Africa, however, that the developments in this direction have been most notable. All the universities formed in the formerly British territories of Sierra Leone, Ghana and Nigeria have departments of religion, as have Makerere and Nairobi in East Africa. Progress in Dar-es-Salaam in Tanzania seems for the time being to be held up by the doubts felt by the large Muslim minority. Malawi seems to be headed in the direction of a department. All these have, of course, to be departments of what used to be called 'comparative religion', a term still in common use among laymen, though experts abandoned it a good many years ago.

Even the more thoughtful Roman Catholics are of the opinion that too many years in a seminary are not a good thing. They would prefer to see students do two preliminary years in seminary, then three years of general religion in a department of religion in a university, and finally come back for two years or more of professional training in a seminary. In view of the extreme conservatism which prevails in many sections of the Roman Catholic Church, it must be regarded as unlikely that so radical a change will come about in any near future. It is interesting that progressive opinion seems to be moving in this direction. And, outside the Roman Catholic Church, opposition to such a policy is likely to be less rigorous.

We have not yet moved far away from existing situations and forms of training. But more radical questions will not be denied a hearing.

Do we in fact need a full-time ministry at all?[6] There has been much discussion in recent years of tent-making ministries. No one has ever denied that churches can make use of such ministries, and flourish under the care of part-time ministers, if no other form of ministry is available. During the second world war practically every Japanese pastor in order to survive had to take some other job in addition to that for which he had been ordained. If such action has to be taken again, we will take it, and believe that the Lord of the Church will see to it that no great harm comes to the life of his people. But the general experience of the Church over nineteen centuries points in the other direction. Part-time ministries must be regarded as supplementary. Their effectiveness depends in large measure on their being linked to a supply of fully-trained and full-time ministers. This is by no means to say that the door to ordination should be closed to those who are eager to serve in this way and have the necessary gifts. But to imagine that a supplement can become a substitute is sheer illusion.

That is the first question. The second asks whether we need residential seminaries. Can one not learn far better on the job?

[6] This question was raised again at the Nairobi Assembly in 1975, in the report of the section which dealt with education. It had already been extensively discussed at the Tambaram Missionary Conference of 1938.

The fundamental error in a great deal of training with a view to ordination has been the assumption that if a student has spent a certain number of years in an institution of theological learning and has passed a certain number of examinations, he will be fitted to engage at once in the delicate work of the Christian ministry. Nothing could be further from the truth. The cure of souls is a far more delicate art than the cure of bodies. To be a minister of religion is far more difficult than to be a physician or surgeon. The medical student, having passed his final examinations is then expected to serve for a period as house physician and house surgeon under expert guidance, before being let loose on his own to kill or cure. The same custom prevailed until recently in the ministry of many churches. In many areas, such as Christian education or pastoral care, some general principles can be learned in seminary. But the job can be learned only in *doing* the job. Therefore ordination was followed by a period as curate or assistant to some more experienced man who was supposed to distill from the depths of his experience such further wisdom as the fledgeling might be supposed to require. Whatever other reforms may be made, not much progress is to be expected until the first four years after ordination are regarded as a period of further training under authority.

When, however, the question of in-service training is raised, the meaning is usually something rather different from this. Is it not possible for the candidate for ordination to get the whole of his training while engaged in the job by which he earns his living, whether that be an ordinary secular avocation, or some occupation in the service of the Church which does not carry with it the privileges and burdens of the ordained ministry? Some advantages of such a method are obvious without extended discussion. The candidate will spend his days in contact with ordinary people and their needs, avoiding the isolation from everyday life which is inevitable in a seminary. His gifts and aptitudes can be tested out far more thoroughly and searchingly than through the rather artificial testing of academic life. It is also believed that this method is financially much less demanding than that of institutional training.

Long second thoughts are in order at this point. If men and women of comparatively little education are to study on their own, the necessary materials must be carefully prepared. Such preparation is not an easy task. A beginning has been made. The results so far brought under observation suggest that they provide far too much spoon-feeding and underestimate the native intelligence of those for whom they are intended. Tuition by correspondence is one of the most expensive forms of education that has ever been invented. Constant visits to students are essential if they are not to suffer from a sense of isolation – isolation not from the needs of ordinary men but from the centres of learning and the companionship of fellow students. And, for all the criticisms that we have made, the seminary is not an unmitigated evil. Fellowship with other students and with teachers is an essential part of any form of theological training. The experience of living the liturgical life with others over a period of months rather than weeks can be dispensed with only at the cost of weakening the whole process of training. Even 'these buildings' can be put to good use, if they are kept simple and related to the kind of life to which students will return. And when those who have undergone this kind of training have been launched upon their work, they will need more, not less help and guidance than those who have followed what up to now has been regarded as the normal method of training.

It would be unwise to overlook the difficulties and weaknesses attendant on this as on all methods of training. It seems, however, that this is likely to become increasingly the accepted pattern. It has already been taken up enthusiastically in several regions of the world, especially in Latin America. If those who have been engaged in it are to be believed, success is considerable, and the advantages greatly outweigh the drawbacks. We shall await with interest reports from one diocese in Kenya which has committed itself to 'in-service training'.

But, when we have considered all possible methods of training for the ordained ministry, we have still left out about half of our subject. Where does the layman come in?

4. Where Does the Layman Come In?

We have been told many times by observers that in the past missionaries have bedevilled the situation in the third world by introducing a purely western type of ministry which does not suit the mentality of these newer and less-developed churches,

114

and imposes on them financial burdens which they are not able to bear.

As far as the urban churches are concerned there may be some substance in this charge. With the steady growth in urbanization in all these areas and especially in Africa, where the rate of increase is reckoned to be five per cent per annum,[7] such churches gain in importance. Every one of such congregations expects to have a full-time minister of its own. His status in the community and the kind of work that he is expected to do put him very much on the same level as his opposite number in a western church. If he is in charge of two hundred families, and each family is prepared to give one per cent of its income for the support of its minister, there will be no financial problem: the minister will be twice as well off as the average among his parishioners (as was the parish priest of the medieval village[8]), and this means that he will be relatively better off than his peers in other parts of the world.

The churches of the third world are, however, overwhelmingly village churches. And here the type of ministry which has grown up is as different as could be imagined from the patterns familiar from the traditions of the west. The priest of an English village in the Middle Ages found himself in charge of that one village of perhaps two hundred souls, and of nothing else. The ordained minister in East Africa may find himself charged with the oversight of twenty village congregations scattered over an area the size of one of the smaller English counties.

Many students of missions will say emphatically that this ought never to be allowed to happen. They would subscribe to the views so persuasively put forward by Roland Allen[9] in a series of books, that each Christian group should from the start be made complete in itself with elders ordained to celebrate the Lord's Supper, and so to make available and without special effort the full ministry of the word and sacraments. Allen had

[7] See the *South African Journal of African Affairs*, vol. 4, no. 1, table 3, page 7.

[8] In the division of land for cultivation the parish priest was ordinarily given two strips, whereas the common parishioner had to be content with one.

[9] See the article by N. Q. King in the *Concise Dictionary of Christian World Mission*, ed. Neill, Anderson and Goodwin (Lutterworth Press, 1970), pages 14–15.

been a missionary in China. He nowhere deals with the problems that arise when all the converts are illiterate, as was the case in many parts of Africa, and as is still the case among the scheduled castes in India. Nor did he take into account the many social pressures to which, as a result of the caste-system, Christians of the less privileged classes are subjected in India. But his ideas are gaining ground. He himself maintained that he was a prophet fifty years before his time. It is possible that a revolution along the lines that he suggested may take place before the end of the twentieth century, and that his writings may be found more relevant to the situation that will then obtain in the Church than they were at the time of their first appearance.

If we take as our starting-point the situation as it exists today, I see no reason to change the words I wrote in 1950 in the first report I prepared for the International Missionary Council on theological training in Africa: 'The village catechist, with his slender qualifications and very modest pay, is the real hero of the Christian situation in Africa'. Judging by the situation as I have observed it over the last five years in East Africa, it seems to me likely that the words will still be relevant at the end of this century.

The Commission on Theological Training of the Anglican Province of Kenya, of which I had the honour to be chairman, found that there were in the Province about two hundred ordained priests engaged in pastoral work, and not less than sixteen hundred village catechists, also called church teachers, lay readers or evangelists, charged with carrying out most of those duties of teaching, preaching and conducting services which in older churches are the responsibility of the ordained minister. The great majority of these men had received no training at all for the work that had been committed to them. Thus by far the greater part of the Church's work is carried out by untrained laymen. The work of the ordained minister is supervisory to an extent that is known in the western churches only in certain areas of the Methodist Church. The greater part of the minister's time should be spent in training others to do the detailed work which he will never have time to do himself.

In some areas the situation is worse than it was fifty, or even a hundred years ago.

In the days of rapid growth in South India, the missionaries devised what came to be known as the Tinnevelly system, which must be regarded as having been almost ideally suited to the period in which it held sway. Almost all the 'agents' were village schoolmasters as well as catechists.[10] Every month they were required to come in for two whole days to the centre where the missionary resided. There they received their scanty pay; but that was the least important part of the operation. Several hours were spent in careful Bible teaching, in the local language, of course. One of the catechists preached a sermon which was then discussed by all present, probably with a considerable measure of frankness. Every problem of village life was discussed and questions of church discipline were settled. A man who had had twenty years in service would have attended something like two hundred of these sessions, and would have received a very thorough grounding in biblical theology and in the work of the ministry. Such men knew that they might in due course be chosen for the higher course in theology which would lead on to the work of the ordained ministry. Similar – though rather less elaborate – methods have been reported from other areas in corresponding periods of church growth.

Now all is changed. In Kenya, for example, all the schools (the majority of which up to 1966 were mission schools) have been taken over by the government. Religious teaching is permitted, indeed encouraged (perhaps because the government thinks that religious teaching helps to produce docile citizens); but the connexion with the Church is tenuous. In South India, though the schools are still technically church schools, the teachers are appointed and paid by the government. Few indeed are those who feel a vocation to undertake the laborious work of the church as well as that of the school. Already in many parts of the church the work is carried on by lay volunteers. The process of change is likely to continue and the percentage of trained and full-time workers to diminish.

Of the faithfulness of these volunteers it is impossible to speak too highly. Yet their achievements often fall below the hopes of their friends and their own aspirations. The man among them who has had a three weeks' course in a Bible school is regarded as highly trained. Though the production of literature planned to be useful to workers on this level of competence is increasing

[10] The S.P.G. in those days made the delightful distinction between 'pure catechists' and 'mixed agents'.

in the main languages of the third world, it is still pitifully inadequate. My plea for a simple commentary on the New Testament to be published in monthly parts has not been taken up in any language. Many workers do not know what books are available, and are carrying on with nothing in their hands except the New Testament 'without note or comment' in their own language. On the basis of this slender equipment, the Church expects them to preach three sermons in the month, to take classes in preparation for baptism and confirmation, and to attend to financial and other chores. They have to wrestle with the generation gap if their congregation includes sophisticated and cynical boys and girls from high school, or even from college. One cannot but feel deep sympathy in both directions when students coming back from vacation in their homes say, as they are wont to do, 'When we are at home, we cannot go to church; it is simply too awful'. The student feels that he is regarded as an unwelcome intruder. If he does take himself in hand and force himself to go to church, he will find little that appeals to him.

The Commission (to which I have referred) carefully considered the situation of the village churches and of the workers who so faithfully served them. The conclusion of the discussion was that, if the most elementary needs of the situation are to be met, the Province must provide five Bible schools to correspond roughly with the five geographical and linguistic areas into which it can be divided. Each school should have a staff of three full-time and fully qualified theological teachers, one of whom should be mainly itinerant, maintaining contact with those who had received training in the school. It was recognized that great flexibility would have to be observed regarding length and character of courses of training, and that frequently it would be necessary, as suggested by the report from West Irian, for the team to go out to the villages rather than for the village workers to be pulled into the centre and away from jobs which it might be very difficult for them to leave. Much of the time of the teachers would have to be spent in preparing literature of the simplicity required by those who have had no advanced education and no preparation at all in the art of learning for themselves.

It was agreed by the Commission that, in view of the urgency of the need and the lack of qualified theological teachers in the Province, it would involve no departure from the principle of

118

African leadership at all levels, if the need was made known to other Anglican Provinces with an indication that help both in personnel and finance would be welcome, until the time of crisis had passed away.

It has to be recorded with regret that, at the time of writing, the Province has no single Bible school working full-time on the lines suggested by the Commission. Numbers of Christians are increasing rapidly, in some areas to the tune of ten per cent per annum. Educational standards are rising all the time. The provision for the training of workers is perhaps less adequate than it was forty years ago. Some regions in Africa are doing better. Others are doing even worse. These illustrations from one area may give some indication of the immensity of a task which in its modern form the Church has hardly even begun to face.

5. And What of the Sheep?

If the preparation of the shepherds is so inadequate, what is likely to be the situation of the ordinary member of a Christian congregation?

The Roman Catholic expert in African missions, Fr. Adrian Hastings, has warned us repeatedly that we are in danger of bringing into existence all over again the situation created in Latin America by the Spaniards and Portuguese four and a half centuries ago. There mass baptism was the rule. One missionary claimed to have baptized ten thousand people in a single day. But no serious attempt was made after the time of the first bishop Zumarraga (1530–48) to build up an indigenous priesthood.[11] In two centuries of dominance in Paraguay the Jesuits did not bring forward a single Guaraní candidate for the priesthood. When I was in Uruguay a number of years ago, there was one Roman Catholic priest for 8,000 of the population, and in other areas the situation was even more parlous. Recent vigorous initiatives on the part of the Vatican together with the rapid growth of Protestant missions have modified the Latin American situation but have not radically changed it. It is not only in political matters that Latin America continues to be the question mark of the Christian world. Is this the direction in which the Church is heading in Africa, in Indonesia and other areas of rapid Christian advance? It might be well to be warned

[11] See the *Concise Dictionary of Christian World Mission*, page 681.

ahead of time of the perils that are likely to beset us if this is the case.

The first and perhaps the gravest peril is that the Christian faith may take the form simply of a new set of laws to replace the ancient laws that have been abandoned. The heart of man appears to be incurably legalistic. If rules are not provided for him, he will invent them out of his own head. This tendency begins to appear even in the pages of the New Testament, and is clearly marked in the literature of the apostolic age. What began as grace is beginning to turn again into law. It is not surprising that, if the gospel of the grace of God has not been fully and clearly preached, a third-world church living as a minority in a mainly non-Christian world will soon begin to work out its own legalisms. And it is the observance of rules which naturally strikes the outsider. How often in India have we heard non-Christians call out after Christian enquirers, 'Become followers of the way and take a rest on Sundays'. The Sunday rest and the duty of coming to church on Sunday were some of the first things insisted on by missionaries as an outward sign of an inward change of heart. Even more curious are the taboos which have grown up (no one quite knows how) that are more strictly observed than some of the weightier matters of the faith. In some areas in South India it was absolutely forbidden for a woman to pass beyond the communion rail in church, even for so excellent a purpose as cleaning brass flower-vases which after the perfunctory attentions of the mere man might stand much in need of thorough cleaning. If Christianity has once come to be thought of as a legal system, and faith as the keeping of a number of rules, the genuinely devout adherent who is conscious of having kept all the rules may very naturally say, 'What lack I yet?'. To bring the legalist back into the realm of grace is perhaps even harder than to bring the non-Christian into the Christian world in the first place.

What is to be done about all this?

To some leaders in Africa it has appeared that the sovereign remedy for this state of affairs – or prophylactic against it – is to bring back the teaching of African traditional religion into the churches and particularly into the schools. For this there is much to be said. The disintegration of African society is due in part to the over-rapid detachment of the African from his past. It is good that African Christians, no less than others, should be aware of their own past and the excellences that were not lacking in African societies. But the carrying into effect of this excellent plan has presented more difficulties than had been foreseen. What is African traditional religion? There is not one tradition, there are many. How is selection to be made? There are shadows in African tradition as well as lights, and these ought not to be altogether overlooked. Nevertheless it is good that the attempt is being made; early imperfections in implementation may be eliminated by deeper knowledge and more skilful presentation.

Will the introduction of such teaching have the desired effect in the renewal of the African churches? Some confidently affirm that it will; to others the answer is much less self-evident. It is frequently asserted that, whereas the African in his pre-Christian state was religious all the time, Christianity was presented to him as a one-day-in-the-week religion, and therefore never penetrated deeply into his consciousness. Simply as a matter of history this is certainly untrue. The early missionaries in East Africa, whether Roman Catholic or Protestant, were all seven-days-a-week, seven-times-a-day Christians. I have never yet received an answer to the question why the African Christian failed to integrate his faith at every point into the life of the village and the home, as the Indian Christian was so successful in doing. The contrast is deserving of careful study.

In an Indian Christian village, the festivals of the church are the festivals of the village. At the present time interesting attempts are being made to adapt to Christian use such Hindu festivals as *Tibavali*, the festival of lights. It is unlikely, however, that these festivals, if adopted and adapted in Christian use, will displace Christmas, Easter and Harvest Festival, which have so deeply impressed themselves on the Indian Christian consciousness. But in an Indian village, it is not only the regular festivals which link the life of the family to the Christian faith. No Indian Christian would dream of entering into a newly-built house until a service of dedication has been held. Sowing will not start until a basket of rice has been brought to the church and prayed over. The villager would be deeply concerned if even for a single evening the bell did not sound to call the faithful to prayer.

It appears that the experiences of the African Christian have not been the same. The difference may point to the real remedy for the gravest dangers facing the churches at the present time.

The enemy is biblical illiteracy. One major remedy is the New Testament in every hand, and the availability of means to help the Christian and his family to discover what the New Testament is really all about.

The ferment of thought in the Bible Societies of the world is one of the most significant new features on the Christian scene. It is not enough to translate the Bible; it is necessary also to make sure that those who read can answer affirmatively the question which Philip put to the Ethiopian eunuch: 'Understandest thou what thou readest?' (Acts 8:30). The old rigid principle that the Bible must be translated 'without note or comment' has been broken through to the extent that explanatory notes may now be added. This should add greatly to the value of the translations. And the Bible Societies seem prepared to go even further – in the provision of New Readers' Translations, where liberty for paraphrase and adaptation will be given to an extent which would not be acceptable in anything that could strictly be called translation. Much spade-work still needs to be done, and no clear definition has as yet been reached as to the acceptable limits of paraphrase; but we seem to be on the edge of exciting developments – provided always that the new readers themselves do not object to being given something other than 'the real Bible'.

Two cautions should perhaps be interjected.

We who have long been literate tend to underestimate the native intelligence of the illiterate, or of those who have only recently come to literacy. After all, the world of the Old Testament is much nearer to many of them than it is to us. Those troublesome people, the daughters of Zelophehad who keep turning up in the Pentateuch to the perplexity of western readers, present no problem at all to many 'new readers'; they are able at once to understand the gravity of the problem by which these ladies were faced, and how important it was that the right solution should be reached. Such readers have a passionate interest in genealogies as authenticating the validity of all the events that are to follow them. Every African knows, though all too many Europeans in Africa do not, that the land belongs to the ancestors, and that no human being can have more than the user of it. So when the Lord says to Israel in the Book of Leviticus (25:23) – 'The land is mine', the African reader's reaction is – 'Why, of course'.

Secondly, for all our profession of faith in the Holy Spirit, we are all too ready to forget that the true Teacher of the word is the Spirit himself. Of course simple people need help in the reading of the Scriptures, the help of those who are prepared to be servants of the word and bring forth for the illumination of the lay Christian things new and old. But all such teaching is vain unless the fire of the Spirit is present to make the ancient words living words in the apprehension and the imagination of the reader today.

Not long ago I had the privilege of visiting the great centre of the Wycliffe Bible Translators in Papua–New Guinea,[12] and there saw work going forward in the language of a people who number only about a thousand all told. The translators think that they may sell five hundred copies; my young German companion gave it as his opinion that they will be lucky if they sell as many as three hundred. I thought that he, with all the weight of western theological scholarship on his shoulders, might be a little contemptuous at the sight of so much labour, without direct aid from Greek and Hebrew, going into a translation for so small a people. I was happy and grateful when he said to me, 'Just think what it could mean when a people like that sit down with the word of God in their own language, to work out what that word means for them today'.

So it seems that we have a chain of teaching and being taught, reaching from the highest to the lowest. Traditionally the bishop, as the guardian of the faith, had a special responsibility for knowing the word of God, and for passing on that knowledge (in its relevance to his own day) to his clergy, in order that they in their turn might pass it on to others. But, in the situation in which we find ourselves today, the clergy themselves have to be trained in such a way that they can be teachers of teachers. Already in the twentieth century we have seen the dawning of the day of the layman in the church. The twenty-first century may see noonday come. More than ever before, the work will be done by the devoted and appointed layman in the church. When the minister has done his work of passing on the truths of the gospel to the men and women around him who have no special office in the church, we might think that the chain of

[12] These pioneers are working at present in a hundred-and-one Papuan languages. There are still more than two hundred in which no work has as yet been started.

communication had come to an end. But this is by no means the case. There are always those 'who are without', either in the sense that they do not know the gospel at all, or that they have failed to discover its meaning or have lapsed from an earlier allegiance. To such the ordinary layman often has better access than the professional. And then there is always the coming generation to be borne in mind. In this book there has been no room to do more than mention the enormous significance of the Christian family, 'the church that is in thy house'. The fathers to the children must declare the wonderful works of God, and to this process there will be no end until the kingdom of God comes with power. Every teacher must be a learner, and every learner must be a teacher.

So perhaps at the end of the chapter, we come to Chaucer's exquisite summary of the attitude of the poor scholar:

And gladly would he learn and gladly teach.

6

GREATER THINGS THAN THESE

1. Prophets in Peril

The title of our study is 'Salvation Tomorrow'. We have had to take some glances backwards into that past out of which the present has been born, and outwards to that present in which the germs of the future lie hidden. We have noted that at certain points the ecumenical movement seems to have become imprisoned in a past which is no longer with us, and has to some extent abandoned its prophetic rôle in intense concentration on contemporary problems. Our interest, however, has throughout been in the future. In what direction is the finger of God pointing? Can we in a measure discern the signs of the times in which the outlines of a still hidden future can be discovered? Now the time has come at which that unknown future has to be the primary concern of our enquiry; we have to engage in the dangerous task of prophecy.

At all times there are many prophets in the world. Some of them are false and some of them are true. How is the one group to be distinguished from the other? The prophet is always at risk. He can offer in advance no credentials other than his own certainty of the truth of the message that he has to deliver. But conviction is not the same thing as credibility; anyone who sets out on the dangerous road of prophecy knows well that one day he may be proved to have been wrong. This is a risk that cannot be avoided.

The nature of this risk may be indicated by drawing attention to some prognostications which have been made in the Christian world, and which do not seem to be advancing towards fulfilment.

If we look only on the dark side of happenings in the Christian world in our day, it is only too easy to be discouraged, and perhaps even to think that we have committed ourselves to the support of a falling cause. There are among Christians a number of professional pessimists who seem to regard it as their calling to spread alarm and despondency in the Christian ranks, instead of encouraging the quiet confidence which is based not on immediate advantage but on the faithfulness of God.

In recent years we have been told a great many times, in a number of reputable Christian publications, that Muslim missions have been much more successful in Africa than Christian missions, and that five times as many people are becoming Muslims in a year as are becoming Christians. This has been endlessly repeated. On what evidence, if any, is this discouraging statement based?

Personal investigation, as far as I have been able to carry it out, lends no support to it whatever. In Rhodesia Islam is practically unknown, except for a small number of immigrants mostly of Pakistani origin. The same is true of Zambia. Over the greater part of Zaïre, that vast area in the very heart of Africa, Islam exercises hardly any influence at all. It is found in some strength only in the north-eastern part of the country, which has a common frontier with the Sudan, a predominantly Muslim country. In Kenya Muslims form an old and highly respected minority, forming perhaps eight per cent of the population.[1] But, whereas in some areas Christian progress is measured at the rate of ten per cent per annum, there seems to be no area in which Islamic advance takes place at anything like a comparable rate. The same is true in Uganda, except that there the Muslim population does not exceed five per cent. In eastern Nigeria there has been great activity in the building of mosques; but the land has already been so extensively Christianized that the increase in the number of Muslims does not seem to have kept pace with the increase in the number of mosques.

Where, then, are the great successes of the Islamic missions to be found? It is reasonable to suppose that in certain areas, mostly in the former French colonies, Islam is on the march; but nowhere is there evidence of gains on the gigantic scale indicated by the statement mentioned above.

Islam is a power in Africa, and will certainly continue to be so. It is possible, however, that its attractive power is less than it was a generation or two ago. Africa has become more aware than it was of the connexion between Islam and slavery. Of the six main slave-trading routes, only two were operated by the

[1] The *Kenya Churches Handbook* (1973) suggests that a more accurate figure would be slightly less than seven per cent.

white man, whereas four had been for centuries an appanage of Islamic power, with some participation by the Portuguese in the Zambesi area. Of course white man and African and Arab all shared in the guilt of that infamous traffic. But there has never been a Muslim movement for the abolition of slavery parallel to the western and Christian effort which has resulted in the almost total disappearance of slavery from the African continent.

It may be that Islam is not offering the kind of progress which Africa is avidly seeking in the twentieth century. Technology is in the air; the African believes that with a right use of the resources available to him, he can pass from the poverty of the past into an era of prosperity. But where should he go to seek the technological expertise without which this dream cannot become actuality? Thousands of African students go to Russia and to Eastern Germany, with Western Germany, Britain and the United States as less successful competitors in the race. Very few by comparison are those who go to an Islamic country. Arabic is a great and noble language. But who learns it today, other than those who intend to become teachers of Islam, or who have special antiquarian or linguistic interests? The brotherhood of Islam is still a great reality. But the African, now regarding himself as a citizen of the world, perhaps feels less need than he did for this more restricted fraternity.

This is not the only discouraging statement purveyed by the Christian pessimists. There is a second. This is to the effect that, though the number of Christians in the world is increasing, the Christian percentage of the whole is decreasing all the time. Twenty years ago, we are informed, the Christian proportion of the world's population was about one third; by A.D. 2,000 when the total population will have doubled in number, Christians will make up not more than a sixth of the whole. This is the form in which the statement is usually made; but I have seen in one source the Christian share put as low as ten per cent.

As far as I know, no detailed account has ever been given of the data on which these statements are based, or of the calculations which have led to these conclusions. When evidence is collected and sorted, it seems to point in a very different direction.

In the first place, Christians have a share in the population explosion no less than those of other faiths or of no faith at all. Indeed in a number of areas the survival rate among Christians, as a result of greater attention to hygiene and better ante-natal care, is rather higher than among non-Christians. Even allowing (as we must) for substantial defections from the Christian ranks, there is no reason to suppose that these would reach such proportions as to reduce by half the Christian percentage of the world's population.

Moreover, in addition to natural increase by the excess of births over deaths, we have to reckon with the continual process of conversion from the non-Christian faiths. How is this likely to affect projections for the future?

The most careful calculations so far have been carried out by D. B. Barrett and the Unit of Research at Nairobi. The first step was to obtain from the United Nations and similar international organizations the most reliable predictions of population growth that could be obtained. Demographic projection is always a hazardous business since the imponderables are so many, and what actually takes place may differ considerably from the estimates. But, in this field, these are the best materials available for this kind of work. The next step was to study carefully the statistics of baptisms and church growth put out by churches and missions in various parts of the world. Church statistics are notoriously inaccurate and have to be used with a good deal of critical caution. But if so used, they can serve as an indication of trends, the reality of which can hardly be denied. On the basis of such evidence Dr. Barrett came to the conclusion that, for Africa as a whole, to an average birth-rate of 3·1 per cent must be added an average conversion rate of 3 per cent per annum. If this continues till the end of the century, the Christian population will by then have quadrupled itself, and will have reached a figure of more than 300 million. Even when allowance is made for a considerable drop in the Christian figures in communist-controlled countries and in increasingly secularized Europe and North America, it seems clear that the Christian percentage of the world's population has increased, is increasing and is likely to continue to increase until the end of this century.

Some may be inclined to say that statistics prove nothing, and that mere numerical advance can give no indication of any reality of Christian progress, since that is an inward and hidden thing, depending on the depth of inner conviction and not on any formality of outward profession. This can hardly be a matter of controversy. But since the Christian pessimists have chosen statistics as their weapon, it seems only reasonable to call their bluff, to subject their statistics to careful analysis and to substitute for them a different set of statistics, of the same kind but based on more careful attention to reality.

As is known to every student of Church history, the Church of Christ has enjoyed no story of unbroken success and no period of universal peace. Persecution has always been in operation somewhere, and there have always been set-backs to balance progress. The gap between profession and attainment has always been immense. And yet the Church continues to exist, and has over and over again given evidence of unlimited capacity for reform and renewal of its inward life. Bishop J. B. Lightfoot's well-known remark that the study of history is a cordial for drooping spirits is not always self-evidently true. But anyone who will look back a thousand years and consider the state of the Church in the year of grace 976 will hardly be able in 1976 to prevent cheerfulness from breaking in. This is not a time, any more than any other time, for facile optimism; but equally it is no time for pessimism, for supposing that the resources of the Church have dried up and that nothing remains but to sit with folded hands waiting for the coming of the day of doom.

2. What Next?

The main successes of the Christian mission over the past two centuries have been won among the technically less advanced peoples of the world, and among those who have had no splendid edifice of ancient philosophy with which to confront Christian aggression as it has come upon them from the west.

Harsh critics of the missionary enterprise have not been lacking. In India it has not rarely been affirmed that this was deliberate policy on the part of the missionaries: they chose the easier path of going to the simpler and more credulous elements in the population and postponed to a future which never came the harder enterprise of approaching the educated and religiously advanced. It would not be easy to support such a criticism on the basis of actual history. Protestant missions have never been distinguished by having any plan at all. But simply as a matter of history the majority of them have followed Robert de Nobili, the famous Italian Jesuit (in India: 1606–52), in going first to the higher castes in the hope and expectation that these when converted would become the elect witnesses to their own

129

people, and that Christian faith would seep downwards from above. In 1830 Alexander Duff founded his famous school in Calcutta with the expressed intention of reaching the higher castes, and with a success that shook Hindu society in Bengal to its foundations. The famous pundit Johnson of the Church Missionary Society in Benares spent his life learning Sanskrit so well that he could speak it as well as any Hindu scholar. His successor W. D. P. Hill, at one time senior classic at Cambridge, gave his life to work in a school for high-caste Hindu boys, and, with typical Cambridge reluctance to commit himself to print, left hardly any memorial to his profound scholarship except his outstanding edition of the Bhagavad Gita, now once again in print.

When movements among the so-called depressed classes in India broke out quite unexpectedly, rather more than a century ago, the missionaries were considerably perturbed. Was this what they had come to India to do? When so many were pressing into the church could personal conversion be looked for? And could any true Christian development be expected if converts continued to live, as perforce they must, in the midst of their non-Christian neighbours? In Burma it was not the missionaries who sought out the less advanced Karens, but the Karens who sought out the Baptists, and to some extent diverted them from their original intention of winning the Buddhists to the faith. It was only gradually that the missionaries became convinced that they were being providentially shown *Christ's Way to India's Heart*[2] and yielded to what seemed to them to be necessity. But as late as the 1930's many Indian Christians of higher caste were still unconvinced and regarded the fostering of such movements as a betrayal rather than a proclamation of the gospel.

Is it necessary to suppose that the missionaries were always wrong in following what seemed to be the path of opportunity? In 1949 the communist take-over in China resulted in the closing of all doors to foreign Christian service in that country. The Roman Catholics immediately turned their attention to Africa, with such massive intensity that in many areas Roman Catholic missionaries outnumber all the Protestant forces together by ten to one, and that although the Roman Catholics came late upon

[2] This is one of the two classic works by the Methodist Bishop J. W. Pickett, the other being *Christian Mass Movements in India*.

the scene, in almost all African territories their adherents now constitute the largest of all Christian bodies. Were they perhaps wiser in their generation than the Protestant missions? May entering rapidly into open doors prove to be a wiser strategy than shedding futile tears over those which have been closed?

Military metaphors are not in fashion these days, but at times the Church might have something to learn even from the despised art of military strategy. The simple hard-hitting officer tends to imagine that the way to win a war is for everyone to be fighting simultaneously all along the front. The back-room boys (perhaps shrewder) know that the simple facts of logistics make this impossible, that the defence always has the advantage over the attack, and that the apparently simple approach to victory is in point of fact the best way to lose a war. Warfare involves the ceaseless probing of the enemy's defensive structure in order to find the weak spots in it, and the concentration of increased strength just at the point at which a breakthrough may be possible. Something similar may be observed in the history of the Church.

The movement of the gospel in history seems generally to have been from below upwards rather than from above downwards. There are, of course, exceptions. In northern Europe in many cases the ruler was converted first and the subjects docilely followed him into the Church. The quality of the resulting Christian faith does not suggest that this was the ideal method of procedure. Paul seemed to hit the nail on the head when he wrote that 'God chose what is foolish in the world to shame the wise, God chose what is weak in the world to shame the strong, God chose what is low and despised in the world, even things that are not, to bring to nothing things that are' (1 Cor. 1:27–28, RSV). Following his lead, we need not be too much dismayed if in the past two centuries God has used the Church to bring into the fellowship of his kingdom those peoples or parts of peoples which are inferior only in the sense that they had not yet been introduced into the world of modern technology, and that they had not been in a position to exercise extensive political, social or economic power.

Nor need we be over-anxious if for the moment the main openings for Christian witness are in countries where, though political independence has been achieved, social disintegration has disrupted old patterns, literacy is at a low level, and the

131

Church may be able to commend itself as having at least in some degree the power to rebuild what has been cast down and to find new patterns to replace the old. There are areas which have refused to admit any foreigners for the purposes of Christian service. But, apart from such exceptions, there is little doubt that, if the churches really set themselves to the task, the evangelization of these peoples could be completed before the last quarter of this century has run its course.

Let us look a little more closely at Africa. South of the Sahara there are something like 750 peoples (the term 'tribe' is no longer acceptable) each with its own language and culture. According to a recent survey, the results of which had been made available to the Lausanne Assembly of 1974, there is hardly one among these peoples which has remained wholly untouched by the influence of the gospel. But the level of penetration varies from almost complete Christianization, as is the case with some of the peoples of Uganda, to rare and superficial contacts. Careful investigation in West Africa brought to light a people a million strong in the former French colony of Dahomey, and an even larger people in the Upper Volta region, among whom (though there were some Christian centres) the great majority of the population were without any opportunity of hearing the name of Christ. The French-speaking Presbyterians in West Africa felt that this was a challenge which could not be overlooked. An enterprise called the *Action Apostolique Commune* was brought into being with a view to pioneer work in Dahomey. An international team of French-speaking Protestants was brought into being with representatives from countries as remote from one another as France, Tahiti and Madagascar. Results have not so far been commensurate with hopes. It seems that the initial difficulties of pioneer work in an unknown country had been underestimated, and that inadequate care had been given to the preparation of those who were to undertake the work. Long patience is the primary virtue required of those who give themselves to the evangelization of those who have never heard the gospel.

The limited success achieved by one effort should not lead to the conclusion that the attempt was not worth making, or that other similar ventures may not be crowned with greater success. More careful planning and a greater measure of support from existing sources might lead to very different results.

A rapid survey of the available data suggests that there may be in Africa south of the Sahara about a hundred areas (varying in population from ten thousand to two million people) in which so far no continuous witness for Christ has ever been undertaken. Are the resources of the Christian world inadequate for the work of entering into all these areas in the course of the next twenty years? Has Christian co-operation reached the point at which churches would be ready to accept a measure of guidance as to who should go where, and which church should be willing to accept the responsibility for each particular area?

It is easy to draw out theoretical plans for missionary advance and lose sight of the difference between the nineteenth century and the twentieth. In the high days of colonialism western churches took it for granted that, aided by international agreements or by concessions largely extorted by the pressure of western arms, they could go where the Spirit moved them and found missions as and where they liked. The end of colonialism has entirely changed the picture, and in general to the great advantage of the Christian cause. The obligation to preach the gospel to every creature has not been abrogated. But old methods have been radically challenged, and the demand made that new methods be thought out to meet new situations. Moreover, nothing irritates the African or Asian Christian more than the bland assumption that he is no more than a pawn in a western game, and that his destinies may be settled by forces over which he has no control.

If plans for extensive evangelization are to have any chance of success, certain conditions will have to be fulfilled:

1. At every point the fullest consultation must be maintained with third-world churches and those larger units, national Christian councils and so on, into which increasingly they are grouped.

2. Mission today is understood in terms of approach to the whole man in his total setting. Evangelism is from the start under suspicion if it is understood simply in terms of scattering Christian seed in a soil the nature of which has not been carefully studied in advance.

3. This means that the fullest advantage must be taken of the progress of ethnological and cultural studies. Every missionary,

whether brown or black or white, should have had adequate training in anthropological method before entering his or her field of labour – this to be renewed at intervals by further periods of study. This process need not involve a watering down of the gospel, or a syncretistic refusal to face the differences that exist between the noblest tribal traditions and the gospel of Jesus Christ.

4. As far as possible such efforts must be from the start under indigenous leadership. This is a condition which can less easily be fulfilled than might be supposed. Churches in all parts of the world are growing so rapidly that the existing leaders are weighed down by burdens too heavy to be borne. In only rare cases can leaders be spared to undertake pioneer work in areas in which they will be in a measure foreigners. It is hard to see how this situation can be remedied in the near future, unless the churches are prepared to consider the pooling of resources in personnel as well as in finances, on a scale that has hardly yet been considered.

5. From the start the aim must be to build a genuinely indigenous church, African or Indonesian or whatever it may be. The lessons of missionary history are there to be learnt. On the one hand, if converts are left too suddenly on their own without adequate grounding in the Scriptures or some experience of what it means to live in a Christian fellowship, the result is likely to be collapse. This is especially the case if the majority of the converts are still illiterate and the Scriptures have not yet been made available in a language which they can read for themselves. On the other hand, too long a period of spoon-feeding by witnesses from outside and over-generous financial support from extraneous sources inhibit progress towards a personal apprehension of the gospel and an understanding of the principle that a church is not fully a church until it can take responsibility for the management of all its own affairs. This means that from the start converts must be involved in the process of decision-making. They may still need guidance from their more experienced friends, but they must learn that the true guide is the Holy Spirit, and that it is for them, through prayer and the study of the written word as it comes to them, to find out what the Spirit is saying to them in their particular situation.

134

6. The missionary, to whatever race or nation he may happen to belong, must consciously guard himself against the illusion of permanence in which so many of his predecessors have become trapped.

It only remains to stress once again the difference between evangelism and conversion. All missionary history shows that ten years are likely to elapse between the beginning of the work and the first baptism, and another ten years before anything like a movement into the church begins to be discernible. The period may be very much longer. The first fifty years of the work of the Church in Kenya (1844–94) were almost barren of results. The next fifty years were a period of hard, back-breaking work, in which results began to show and the form of the church began to appear. Only after the centenary year did what had grown from a trickle into a sizable stream show signs of turning itself into a torrent which in the end would carry all before it. There is no reason to suppose that in areas newly to be brought under the influence of the gospel the result will be markedly different. Reaping is usually preceded by a long period of sowing; the longer the period of sowing, the greater the harvest is likely to be when it comes.

If, however, some such planning as has here been indicated could be adopted by the churches, it should be possible at the end of the century to claim that notable progress has been attained in carrying out the command that the gospel should be preached in such a way as to make disciples of all nations. Some hindrances, perhaps grave ones, must be expected from political changes on the way. The main obstacles to progress are likely to be found elsewhere. There is evident in the 'main-line' churches a certain failure of nerve and unwillingness to engage in new enterprises, though this is less true of some of the newer movements such as Pentecostalism. The younger churches sometimes claim more than they are able to perform, and are unwilling to accept the help of others in the accomplishment of tasks which are still beyond their strength. Perhaps worst of all, churches have shown themselves singularly unwilling to pay attention to advice which might seem to infringe their right just to go their own way. When, after 1948, Indonesia was closed to missionaries from Holland, it was suggested to the Dutch missionary authorities that they might look towards Thailand, a country which had no colonial past, in which the majority of missions were of the Reformed tradition, and in which they might soon feel themselves at home. The suggestion was received with less than enthusiasm. What we have done in the past is what we must do today, and tomorrow, and world without end. And so opportunities come to be overlooked, and work which could have been promptly done has remained undone.

3. Towards the Twenty-first Century

The individual Christian lives always poised on the horns of a dilemma. He must live each day as though it were his last. Yet, at the same time, if he is wise, he must plan as though he would be at least temporarily immortal. The dilemma is shared by the Church. Will the time of the Church be short or long? On the one hand we are bidden to be as servants waiting for their Lord, with no indication as to the time at which he may arrive. On the other hand, all history shows that febrile expectation of the second advent has led to sterility in service.[3] Enterprises hastily undertaken without due thought are rarely successful. Long-term planning is always exposed to the risk that every assumption on which it is based may be falsified by the vicissitudes of history.

What will the twenty-first century be like? One who has lived through the whole of the twentieth century and has experienced all the changes that have made it the most exciting century in the history of the world so far is not likely to return any confident answer to that question. Yet there are certain indications which may be followed up, always with a readiness to recognize the risks to which all prophecy is exposed, and to believe that things may turn out very differently from the best estimates that can be made at the present time.

We may perhaps tentatively identify three tasks for which the Church is being prepared by its Lord at the present time.

1. The first is engagement with the non-Christian faiths at a far deeper level than has been at present attained. We do know much more about one another than we did; but perhaps we have been engaged in conflict about the out-works rather than the central fortresses of faith.

We may with advantage look at what the phenomenologists

[3] The Epistles to the Thessalonians show that this danger was present even in the earliest days of the Church.

have had to say about their own approach to the study of religions. Here is what Hendrik Kraemer had to say about the attitude of his distinguished predecessor at Leyden:

> This phenomenological approach is the effort to understand these areas of culture, e.g. religion, according to their *own* inner meaning and structure . . . the requirement . . . is a scrupulous reverence for the facts and genuinely sympathetic understanding. It is clear that this is something else than a new method of research, which automatically yields results. It is for the true phenomenologist the lifelong *education* in the *right* art of empathy (to use this clumsy translation of the German *Einfühlung*) for the subject of his research.[4]

Einfühlung, to feel your way into something which may in itself be unfamiliar. Here of course feeling has no reference to emotion; it indicates the sensitiveness, the disciplined and instinctive sympathy by which the enquirer is led to intuitive understanding on a far deeper level than that of mere intellectual apprehension.

The same scholar warns us as to the limits set to the type of research which he recommends:

> We cannot become Mohammedans when we try to understand Islam, and if we could our study would then be at an end; we should then ourselves directly experience the reality. The historian seeks to understand, and he is able to do that in an approximate way, approximate but no more. By means of empathy he tries to relive in his own experience that which is 'alien' to him, and that too he can only approximate. Here we see the limit to the validity of historical research. But recognizing the limit of validity is not to deny the value of this research.[5]

These distinguished writers seem to be asking for an impossibility. We must try to understand *from within* any religion which we study; yet it is quite certain that we cannot understand from within any religion other than that to which we ourselves are wholly committed. This is both the hope and the frustration of any serious study of religion; it also explains why Kristensen speaks of the lifelong education of the researcher. We must try to reach ever nearer to our goal, in the knowledge that in its perfection it will always elude us.

[4] In Brede Kristensen, *The Meaning of Religion* (The Hague, 1960), pages xx, xxi.
[5] op. cit., page 7.

Are we then condemned to nothing more than external observation? Is it possible for a Christian to progress some distance in feeling what it is like actually to be a Hindu or a Muslim? One way appears to be open to him, though it is one on which he must enter with considerable trepidation – that of using as his own some of the prayers which have their origin in the world of another faith. A Christian can surely use, with hardly a modification, the *Fatihah*, the great prayer with which the Koran opens and which is constantly repeated by his Muslim friends. He is well aware that this prayer comes to him from a world other than his own familiar world. He knows that he will not interpret it just as his Muslim friend does. But do these two worlds, the Christian and the Muslim, to some extent overlap in the areas of faith and adoration? Similarly the Christian should have little difficulty in making his own the great prayer of the Brihadaranyaka Upanishad:

> From the unreal lead me to the real
> From darkness lead me to light
> From death lead me to immortality.

He is aware that the deliverance for which the devout Hindu pleads is not deliverance in the sense in which the Christian understands the term. Is there not, however, some element of yearning after the ultimate which is common to the Hindu and the Christian? No student of religion will fall into the error of supposing that, because we sometimes use the same words, we mean the same things by them. But does this necessary caution exclude the possibility that there may be here and there a common universe of discourse?

If we can come so far together, the adherent of one faith may courteously ask his friend to consider whether there may not be dimensions in his own faith of which he is not as yet aware, but which are open to his investigation.

That indefatigable student of Islam in its highest manifestations, Bishop Kenneth Cragg, has recently adventured an exploration of this kind at what might seem to be the most sensitive point of Christian-Muslim disagreement, the doctrine of incarnation.[6] Here the Muslim seems to confront Christian affirmation with denial in its most relentless form. But is this

[6] In a composite volume entitled *Truth and Dialogue*, ed. John Hick (London, 1974), pages 126–39.

necessarily the last word on the subject? Bishop Cragg points out, in carefully chosen terms which should give no offence to the Muslim reader, that the koranic concept of revelation does imply a concern of God for man. Why, otherwise, should God have chosen to reveal his will for man in a perspicuous Koran given in the Arabic language? But, if this is so, dare we think that this divine concern might carry God further on the road of self-revelation than we might at first be prepared to allow?

As we have already remarked, it is not always easy to find equally courteous consideration from those invited to take part in a meeting of minds. A letter from a Hindu to a Christian friend is illuminating:

> I am afraid you have minimized your Christ by insisting on the unique claims of Jesus. This absolutization of the conditions of his manifestation in human history, added to a lack of real interiority in the lives of most Christians, is the great stumbling block to us. When you have discovered the inner Christ in the light of the Spirit within, then we shall gladly come forward to share with you our own experience of the interiority of God.[7]

The Christian reader must not allow himself to be put off by the unpleasantly arrogant tone of this letter. The writer, justifiably from his own point of view, is making confrontation impossible; he demands that Christianity should strip itself of everything that makes it specifically Christian in order to accommodate itself to the wishes of the adherent of another faith.

We have to recognize that the warfare of ideas is going on all the time and that in that warfare there is no truce. We are all, whether we will or not, engaged in it. Its progress is of course hidden and unseen; it remains nevertheless the great reality. The philosopher A. N. Whitehead, in his intensely interesting book *Adventures of Ideas* (Free Press, 1953), studies this mysterious process of hidden change. He works out the theory that ideas have their *kairos*, their appointed moment of emergence from long incubation into general consent, when they become part of the accepted furniture of the human mind. He takes the rather obvious example of slavery. How was it possible that so evidently unchristian an institution could last so long, and be so widely accepted as inevitable even by Christians? Why

[7] Letter from Sivendra Prakash, quoted in *Dialogue Between Men of Living Faiths*, ed. S. J. Samartha (WCC, 1973), pages 27–28.

was it that only in the nineteenth century did slavery become intolerable to the conscience of western man?

Can similar changes take place, by some slow and mysterious process, within a religious system? The answer appears to be that the same law is in operation in this field also. We seem to be seeing something of a change of this kind at work within Hinduism. Hinduism presents itself as variable, flexible, but in essence unchangeable. Yet one remarkable change seems to be manifesting itself in the new preoccupation with history and its significance in the writings of a number of Hindu philosophers. Traditionally Hinduism has not been much interested in history, since the events of history take place in the world of *Maya*, illusion, in which no true knowledge and no deliverance are to be found. There was no tradition of history-writing in India until Islam became a power in the land and brought with it that tradition of concern for history which the Arabs themselves had learned from the Greeks. Contemporary India has a deep sense of historical destiny, and a concern for the making of history as well as for the writing of it. Will this lead to a deep rethinking of a number of Hindu ideas, and so to an unconscious *rapprochement* with the thought of the west?

It is possible to arrive by way of compromise at a somewhat easy co-existence of different political and economic systems, and even of different systems of ideas. But in the end, the warfare of ideas does not admit of any such compromise; if one thing is true, its opposite cannot also be true. An inner coalescence may have taken place; then agreement may take the place of confrontation. But it cannot be assumed that this will always be the case.

The clearest case of radical confrontation at present is between the Christian and the Marxist worlds. Marx put forward his famous definition of religion as the opium of the people as long ago as 1843–44. Lenin reaffirmed the dictum in 1908, and expanded it into the remarks: 'Marxism regards all present-day religions and churches and all sorts of religious organizations as organs of bourgeois reaction, aimed at the preservation of exploitation and the confusion of the working class.' As recently as 1957 the philosopher Hermann Scheler expressed much the same idea: 'Religion is able to exercise its class function in the perpetuation of the oppressed class by keeping men in ignorance, superstition and fear, and by destroying the confidence of the masses in their own strength, and by preaching helplessness in the face of the divine will'.[8] These Marxist diatribes are directed against religion in general. But, since Marxism is in origin a European and western faith, it is against Christianity that the full venom of its attacks has been directed.

We have stressed more than once the duty that rests on Christians to attempt to understand Marxism, and to recognize the measure of truth that may be found in some of its anti-religious affirmations. But when we have done all that is possible, we may find ourselves faced with irreconcilable antinomies; honesty forbids that we should attempt to equate principles which are, in fact, contradictory of one another.

When we have advanced so far, we may reach the point which has been forcibly described in some notable words of Professor Rudolf Otto, who can hardly be accused of any unwillingness to see the best in every form of religion:

A gigantic struggle is developing. Its climax however will only be reached when mankind has reached a certain equilibrium in social and political affairs . . . That will be the highest and the holiest moment in the history of man. It will no longer be a question of political structures, economic groupings or social interests. For then the religions of mankind will arise against one another. After preliminary skirmishings over mythological forms, accidental events of history and the inadequacies common to us all, then at last the struggle will assume its full majestic form. Spirit will arise against spirit, ideal against ideal, experience against experience. And then each and every one of us will have to stand up openly and confess what he has in him that is authentic and profound – if indeed he has anything to show at all.[9]

What has the Christian to show that is authentic and profound? Do religions die out? The clear answer given by history is that they do. Zeus and Ares and Aphrodite have no worshippers today; they have had their day and gone. The removal of the

[8] Quotations from H. G. Koch, *The Abolition of God* (SCM Press, 1963), pages 57, 58.

[9] This quotation has become known to me as preserved by Professor Gustav Mensching; I have not been able to trace it in Otto's published works. Rudolf Otto became world-famous through his work *The Idea of the Holy* (Eng. trans. 1923), but in many other works also he worked towards mutual understanding between religions. It is this that gives special significance to the quotation.

statue of Victory from the Senate in Rome (first under Constantius, d. 361, a second time under Gratian, d. 383) did mark the end of an era. We collect information about the religion of the ancient Britons and the Germans from fragmentary sources. We may regret that it is so but nothing can reverse the verdict of history. These religions have disappeared almost without trace. The Marxist is convinced that in just the same way Christianity will die out and disappear. The Marxist may, of course, be right; it is permitted to the Christian to entertain the supposition that he could be wrong.

2. The second task assigned to the twenty-first century is likely to be the confrontation of the third-world churches with the gospel on a deeper level than that on which so far it has taken place.

A visit to the Battak country in northern Sumatra is for the Christian visitor a memorable experience. Missionary activity among these hardy and attractive people started unpromisingly, the first missionaries Lyman and Munson having been killed and eaten by the inhabitants almost before they had begun their ministry. But with the arrival of Ludwig Ingwer Nommensen (1862), one of the greatest figures in the whole history of the Christian mission, the situation began to change. In the course of his fifty-seven years of ministry, Battak-land began to take on the semblance of a Christian country. Today almost every village has its Christian church. In the area of original penetration almost the entire population is Christian. The musical Germans brought their music with them and taught the Battaks to sing their faith as well as to profess it. In the Karo Battak area, much more recently opened up, Christian progress is as rapid as in any part of the world. A small number of foreigners are still in service; but control and direction are entirely in the hands of Battak leaders.

Outwardly everything is as good as it could be. But an inner questioning will not be stilled. Are these people Christian Battaks or are they Battak Christians? Is this a distinction without a difference? A little elucidation will make clear a problem that is applicable in a great many areas besides that in relation to which we have raised the question. Are these folk Battaks who have retained almost entire their ancient structure of thought and ways of living, adding to them a certain number of Christian ideas and ways of doing things? Or are they believers who through Christ have accepted an entirely new life-structure, but have retained within this structure such elements of Battak life as are not incompatible with the Christian principles that they have absorbed? This is the crucial question.

Missionaries are constantly being accused of having destroyed ancient structures and wantonly rejected everything that belonged to the pre-Christian past of their peoples. There is a measure of truth in this complaint, but it does not seem to apply to the situation in the Battak country. The Rhenish missionaries were deeply impressed by the Battak *adat* – that highly complicated system of relationships, duties and prohibitions with which the people had lived for centuries, and by which the pattern of their life had been determined. As the Church grew, the missionaries decided to retain the *adat* as far as possible untouched, and to leave it to the Battak people themselves to determine what things from the past could be kept and what must be abandoned. This was, in theory, a most excellent policy. But what have been its actual effects on the Christian development of these now very large churches?

This question has recently been the subject of careful research carried out by Professor Lothar Schreiner, who after thorough theological training and eight years of missionary work in the Battak country is exceptionally well qualified to undertake such study. His conclusion is that the general effect of the retention of so much from the *adat* has been to soften the impact of the gospel on the people; the result has been co-existence rather than confrontation. Parts of the gospel have never been really heard. On the deepest levels of his being the Battak is still a Battak; his reactions, especially in times of crisis, are likely to be determined by the ancient traditions rather than by the teachings of the Lord whom he has more recently come to know.

In a recent number of the periodical *Theologia Viatorum*[10] D. Crafford published a most interesting study of religious attitudes of Christian students in the Black University of the North at Turfloop in the Northern Transvaal. Dr. Crafford first cites from the Dutch periodical *Wereld en Zending*[11] the opinion of the Nigerian scholar and historian Dr. E. A. Ayandele that

[10] Vol. II, no. 1, June 1974, pages 20–34.
[11] *Wereld en Zending*, no. 5, 1972, pages 388–94.

with a few exceptions, the black Christian of Africa remains 'pagan' in his heart. Christianity is no more than a thin layer of varnish while in the deepest being of the African the traditional religion still predominates. He asserts that it is the traditional that forms the instinctive attitude, ethics and aesthetics, if not the life and world vision, of millions of African Moslems and Christians.

He then goes on to report the result of an enquiry directed at two hundred university students, the majority of whom had grown up in Christian homes, or had been exposed to Christian influences from an early age. Two questions are particularly interesting:

(a) Is it right or wrong to consult the *Naganga-Ngaka* ('witch doctor' is the translation usually given, though many Africans regard this as an inadequate or misleading rendering)? The attitude of the churches is quite definite; such consultation is not permitted. For all that, only 29·5 per cent of the students agreed with the verdict of the Church; 62·5 were of the opinion that such consultation is not wrong.

(b) Do ancestors still play a part in the life of human beings? Here 38·5 per cent gave an affirmative, and 55 per cent a negative answer. The remainder expressed no opinion. No one who has worked in Africa will be surprised by these figures. Indeed the only surprising thing is that so many students are prepared to let the ancestors go. An enquiry carried out in Lesotho, not so far away from the Transvaal, suggests that almost all the girls in a Roman Catholic high school held that the ancestors, whether Christian or non-Christian, still played a very important part in the lives of men: 'They are nearer to God than we are, therefore we naturally turn to them'. It is clear that co-existence rather than confrontation had determined for these students the relationship between their past and their present.

How far can foreigners help in bringing about or promoting such a confrontation as has been desiderated. The answer may well be, 'Not at all'. Certainly an attitude of superior or unsympathetic criticism will debar the foreigner completely from any participation in the quest of the third-world churches for a deeper apprehension of the gospel. But some hints given in the previous chapter may point to the possibility of another and a better way. Voices from all over the third world are crying out for more and better Bible teaching. If the Christian from an older church really is a servant of the word, a spirit-filled expositor of the word of truth, there may yet be a rôle for him to fill, a rôle in which he will be eagerly welcomed. Yet such a teacher with the best will in the world cannot jump out of his own skin. Inevitably he will to some extent be asking western questions and finding western answers to them. He may serve as a helper on the way, but the real renewal will not come until the Asian and the African come to the Bible with their own questions, and under the guidance of the Creator Spirit find the answers which are relevant to their situation. To awaken the spirit of enquiry is always the most important of the tasks of the teacher, and difficult in proportion to its importance. The foreigner may find himself baffled by too great a readiness on the part of his hearers to expect and accept his answers. This is exactly the opposite of what he desires. The true answers can come only when the minds and thoughts of Christian teachers in the third world are so illuminated by the Spirit that they in their turn become interpreters and prophets to their own people.

3. What, then, will be the third great task to which the churches will be called in the twenty-first century? In my judgement it will be that confrontation with ourselves – in the light of the gospel – to which we in the west may and should be challenged by our brethren of the third world.

A great deal of criticism is already pouring in from many quarters upon the churches of the west. But most of this is shrill, ill-informed and uncharitable, and therefore is not heard. There are words which wound and do not heal. Some such words uttered at Nairobi 1975 have received all too wide publicity in the press of the world.

If, in the coming century, these churches reach the hoped for level of maturity, if they accept for themselves on deeper levels the challenge of the gospel and experience it with a freshness which it is hard for older churches to attain, it seems certain that they will come to us not as juvenile critics but as brethren, to ask whether we have ever really exposed ourselves to the gospel of Christ as they themselves have experienced it. This they will then have every right to do; they will be repaying any service that we have been able to render to them by a service of perhaps even greater value.

It is not possible at the present time to forecast exactly what form this challenge would take. I see in imagination four areas in which these brethren might find us particularly vulnerable, and in which they would invite us to take a long, shrewd look at ourselves in the light of the gospel:

(a) The first is the materialism which seems to be taken for granted in all western societies, and which when carried to a certain point is likely to make impossible any apprehension of spiritual reality. The west regards Russia and the United States as contrasted, indeed antithetical societies. From the vantage-point of India the two look very much alike, as only slightly variant examples of the materialism of the west. The United States have done more for the preservation of individual freedom; Russia has done more for the liberation of subject peoples. But in both, the guiding principles seem to be production, pollution and enjoyment; none of these has much to do with the gospel of Jesus Christ.

(b) Next we shall be arraigned for the casual way in which we have taken for granted the continuance of injustice, not only injustice far away in South Africa or North Korea, but in our very midst. In a moving passage in his autobiography Lord Woolton has written of the moment at which it occurred to him to ask the question whether it was really necessary that people should always be poor. The persistence of easily removable inequality is a blot on the record of any society that in any way calls itself Christian. This is not a matter of belonging to one political party rather than another; it concerns the obligation resting on every Christian to be endlessly critical of the *status quo* in the light of Christ's words, and to avoid both the somnolence of easy contentment with things as they are, and the pessimism that affirms that nothing can be done.

(c) More serious still is the allegation that we have wholly failed to produce brotherhood in Christ. The Muslim claims – and not without reason – that the brotherhood of Islam is far better than anything that Christianity has to offer. With two suicidal civil wars to our discredit in this century, there is not much that we can say in our defence. It is perhaps possible to claim that we have improved a little. Anyone who has lived through both the world wars of this century knows that bitterness was far less in the second than in the first, and that the recovery of fellowship in the west was far more rapid in 1945 than it had been in 1918. And the ecumenical experiences of sixty years have had at least a minimal influence in promoting a feeling of fellowship among Christians. There is still a long way to go; at least there have been some signs of new beginnings.

(d) The final count in the indictment may be that, whereas the Marxist looks forward eagerly to the fulfilment of his hopes in the future, the west tends to live too much in the past. If the revolutionary is confronted with the harsher and darker aspects of the revolution from which so much had been expected, he is inclined to say, 'The future will provide our justification'. The westerner is inclined too much to look back to the great achievements of the past, and to suppose that, because there is so much greatness in the civilization to which he has fallen heir, the west must offer the type-design for every possible civilization everywhere and at any time.

It is never an easy thing to hear what the Spirit is saying to the churches in our day. Voices come to us out of the past and are listened to with respect. But it may be that the Lord is saying to the churches today new things that have never been heard before, and it may be that the ancient prophetic words translated into the idioms of today might have implications that would shock us out of all complacency.

This is not to say that all voices are to be listened to just because they are new. This was the error into which the German churches allowed themselves to be betrayed in the days during which Hitler was coming to power. They came to believe that the voice of God was to be heard in the great movements of the day – the recovery of national spirit, the consciousness of being a master-race, and so on. They had to be reminded sharply, in the words of the famous Barmen declaration of 1934, that Jesus Christ and he alone is the Word of God to whom we have to hearken, whether it be in life or in death. The harshest criticisms directed against the utterances of Bangkok 1973 were precisely this – that more attention was paid to the contemporary voices of revolution than to the word of Scripture, and that the gospel presented was rather the gospel according to Mao Tse-tung than that according to Jesus Christ.

To listen is essential. To discriminate is hardly less important; the discerning of spirits is an essential part of Christian equipment. Yet our friends in the third world will not forgive us if we make this an excuse for becoming as the deaf adder that stops her ears against the voice of the charmer, and is not prepared to open them for fear of the possibility that the charmer might on occasions be speaking the truth.

It is a platitude that we live in a world of tensions. The Church cannot remain unaffected by what is happening in the world, and the antitheses 'Conservative-Progressive', 'Ecumenical-Evangelical' are heard more often than is good for us. Tensions are of value, provided that they do not reach a point at which they begin to rend the seamless robe of Christ. These lines are written in the hope that by the end of this century the unproductive processes of mutual criticism will have worn themselves out, and that Christians of different convictions will have realized that they are called to go forward together in the adventurous discovery of new truth.

Such discovery always means a rediscovery of Jesus Christ. He, indeed, is the same yesterday, today and for ever; but the Church at different times has seen him with different eyes, as is evident from the pages of the New Testament itself. We do not see as our grandfathers did. The incomparable service rendered by the liberals of the late nineteenth and early twentieth centuries was that they gave us back the figure of the living human Christ, and this made it possible for us to read the gospels as the story of a man. This is, happily, something that we shall never be able to lose.

Is it too early to hazard some guesses as to the direction in which rediscovery is likely to take place? Five suggestions may be made, in the full consciousness that history may show every one of them to have been wrong.

1. We must recognize afresh the immense originality of Jesus Christ. Under the influence of 'comparative religion' and similar tendencies we have been too much inclined to find parallels to the words of Jesus here, there and everywhere, and to suppose that he can be fitted into the category of prophet, or genius, or religious leader, or whatever we prefer. But this is simply wrong. Jesus cannot be understood in any dimension other than his own. He has called into being a new world of reality, in which only those are at home who call him Lord. When Christians use the word 'God', they mean the Father of our Lord Jesus Christ and nothing else. This is a truth that we forget at our peril.

148

2. We must not evade the inexorableness of Christ. We have tended to present to the world a tamed and amiable Christ, perhaps hoping thus to make him more attractive, but overlooking his own word that he came to bring not peace but a sword. His command 'Follow me' is unconditional, and its very indefiniteness makes it formidable. Neither path nor goal is indicated. But the world that crucified Jesus Christ has not so much changed that it is likely ever to be a comfortable home for the disciple.

3. We may set no limit to the creative power of Christ. To some extent we have realized this to be true in the case of the individual, since we have seen those who have been completely transformed by the indwelling power of Christ. We must expect to see the same creative power at work in nations and civilizations. This does not mean that we are to expect to see the kingdom of God upon earth in all its fullness in our day. It does mean that Christ can be creator only in so far as he is also judge and destroyer. Everything that is false and arrogant and shoddy and distorted must fall before the face of him who is true and humble and real and upright. New things cannot be born until many old things have passed away. The new covenant cannot come until that which has become old and weary has completed its task by the achievement of its own disappearance.

4. We have experienced only in small measure the uniting power of Christ. It is true that the Church is already the most international society on the face of the earth, and that Christians when they meet may experience depths of fellowship such as are hardly encountered anywhere else. But we are rebuked by the surprise which such experiences often engender in us. What should be the normal often comes upon us as the unexpected. And we are challenged to see all these experiences within the Church as only beginnings, and to expect that the Christ who through his cross and resurrection is already the Head of the human race, will manifest that headship on a scale and in a manner which will surpass and confound our present imaginings.

5. What the world seems to need today more than anything else is hope. We tend to etherealize hope, to transfer it far beyond the horizons of the immediate and the actual to a vague region

associated with that mysterious phrase the 'second coming of Christ'. Professor Moltmann in his book *Theology of Hope* (already mentioned) has reminded us that part of the strength of Marxism lies precisely in this – that it gives to its adherents hope for the realization of the kingdom of man in a near and easily imaginable future. Christians cannot entertain Utopian dreams, yet they too have proximate as well as ultimate hopes; we have a right to expect to see at least partial and limited triumphs of Christ in human society and in our world.

We must not, however, yield to the danger of trying to shut Christ up within the limits of our existing church structures; he cannot be so confined. We have learned to see in Jesus of Nazareth not only the fulfilment of the great process of God's revelation of himself to and through Israel, but also as the incarnation of the questing and striving of the whole race of man, stumbling and uncertain, and yet with some dim awareness of the one true God who will not for ever hide himself in the shadows. We have to enlarge our understanding of the truth that in the cosmic Christ, as delineated especially in the Epistle to the Ephesians, everything that is good and true and honourable in any aspiration of man will find its place. How this can be we do not know. But we have the assurance given by the apostle that God has put *all things* in subjection under the feet of Christ, and that it is his purpose to sum up, to gather together, *all things* in the one whom by his infinite power he has raised from the dead (Eph. 1:10; 1:22, 23).

We have insisted more than once that the prophet is always at risk. The reality of the future may be different from that which he has so temerariously ventured to depict. But we have also an assurance in Scripture that hope which is based on the truth of God will not put us to shame (Rom. 5:5). We may venture on the basis of such promises to hope that in the coming century those who are called by the name of Christ, and those whom he is still calling to himself, and those who are already in some way mysteriously linked to him even though they are not as yet called by his name, may go forward together to make the acquaintance of a Christ greater and more majestic than we have ever known.

GENERAL BOOKBINDING CO.

79   4   A

292NY2   340   6132

QUALITY CONTROL MARK